50
SUCCESSFUL
HARVARD
APPLICATION
ESSAYS

50 SUCCESSFUL HARVARD APPLICATION ESSAYS

With Analysis by the Staff of the Harvard Crimson

 St. Martin's Griffin ❧ N E W Y O R K

Library of Congress Cataloging-in-Publication Data

50 successful Harvard application essays: with analysis by the staff of the Harvard crimson.—1st St. Martin's Griffin ed.
    p.   cm.
  ISBN 0–312–20647–X
  1. College applications—Massachusetts—Boston. 2. Harvard University—Admission. 3. Exposition (Rhetoric) I. Harvard crimson. II. Title: Fifty successful Harvard application essays.
LB2351.52.U6A13   1999
378.1'616'097446—dc21   99–15304

10   9   8   7   6   5   4

Contents

Songs of Experience

Molding Identity

Acknowledgments

This book represents an effort by the *Harvard Crimson,* the daily newspaper at Harvard University, to help you with the often challenging process of crafting a self-reflective, engaging, and well-written college admissions essay.

In putting together this book, our central aim was variety. Within these pages you will find essays on a breadth of topics, from Russian politics to bananas, in an assortment of genres, from stream-of-consciousness to monologue. These essays were chosen based on writing, creativity, and voice. Each essay is then analyzed by one of our paper's editors to offer a perspective on what the essay aims to do, how it goes about achieving this goal, its strengths and its weaknesses. With the analysis, our aim was, again, diversity. In all, over twenty *Crimson* staff members—from all areas of the paper from business to news reporting—contributed reviews.

None of the contributors to this book—the authors of the essays and the authors of the analyses—is an expert. They are a collection of people who have been through the process themselves and want to help you in crafting a great essay. In other words, you will find many voices, many of which may contradict one another. Listen to the ones that most resonate with you.

There is no formula to this book, just as there is no formula to writing your college essay. Our hope is that somewhere within these pages you will find inspiration for your work. Ultimately, though, your essay must be your own, just as these essays are the personal efforts of their authors.

Finally, I'd like to thank all those people who helped us make this book a reality: Corinne Funk, who told me this could happen and, then, showed me how; Dawn Lee and Jennifer Lee, for administrative support; Kristen Macnamara, our editor at St. Martin's Press; Georgia Alexakis, who compiled the 16 tips; and, most importantly, all the authors who submitted their essays and the *Crimson* staff members who helped to review them.

Good luck.

Matthew W. Granade
President, 125th guard of the *Harvard Crimson*
Joshua H. Simon
President, 126th guard of the *Harvard Crimson*

16 Steps to Success—That May or May Not Prove to Be Surefire

So you want to write a college admissions essay.

By now you have undoubtedly received a wide range of advice from a wide range of sources: guidance counselors urging you to start early, parents worried about your vocabulary level, English teachers stressing the importance of proper grammar.

At this point you have also probably come to the realization that there is no one foolproof method for writing a winning admissions essay. In fact, much of the advice you have probably been given—and which you will read in this book—will probably contradict itself. Example: "Take a risk. Write about something that will make your essay stand out" versus "Don't take any chances. The admissions committee is looking for a well-written, well-argued essay. You can do that without coloring outside the lines." Another example: "The personal statement is only one part of your application. Don't stress" versus "Revise. Revise. Revise. Proofread. Proofread. Proofread. Draft multiple versions. This is the most important piece of writing you will ever produce."

As you can already see, the whole process can be very confusing. Don't let this discourage you. The most truthful advice that can be offered is that there is no one way to write a successful admissions essay. The essay—in terms of both its content and the manner in which it is written—is like you: unique. You can write about your family trip to Niagara Falls or you can write about meeting the Dalai Lama. You can talk about what a perfect student, brother, friend, and all-around good guy you are, or you can write about the day you threw a temper tantrum after losing the state tennis finals. The beauty of the personal statement is that it is completely personal.

Still, we have pledged to help you, and help you we will, by way of the following steps to writing a good, solid impressive admissions essay. Many of these tips resemble advice your high school English teacher would offer. Others are advice that you may have heard from sisters, brothers, and friends. Some of it might even sound like nagging. It's still worth it for us to repeat them and for you to listen to them.

Here goes:

1. *Relax.* The essay is an important part of the application, but your grades, extracurricular activities, interview, and letters of recommendation are also important. The essay is another piece of the whole package. Just make sure you show them you can write well.

2. *Start early.* Enough said.

3. *Brainstorm* ideas with friends, family members, and teachers. Don't rule out any essay topic because it is not impressive enough, exciting enough, or unique enough. An essay about the summer you spent working at Dairy Queen might be more telling than an essay about the day you discovered the cure for cancer.

4. *Avoid clichés* in your writing and be original in your ideas. Be aware that some ideas—winning the state football/soccer/gymnastics championship—have been done at least a thousand times before you. There's nothing wrong with addressing the thrill of victory and the agony of defeat, but try to be more original. Be memorable.

5. *Steer away from gimmicks.* People have pulled them off, but to do it, you have to do it well. If you're a great cartoonist, send in those comic strips. Or if you are a wonderful poet, go for it. But remember, execution is everything and mediocre doesn't win.

6. *Show. Don't tell.* This basic rule of writing applied when you wrote your fifth grade "My Summer Vacation" composition, and it applies now as well. The best essays—the essays that will not be forgotten—have extraordinary use of detail. Use personal experiences to demonstrate your points. The admissions committee, after all, wants to learn things about you that otherwise would not appear on your résumé or transcripts.

7. *Keep the scale of the story manageable.* Use relevant and specific anecdotes to prove your point. Don't expect to express all the nuances and complexities of what the death of a loved one meant in less than 500 words. Keep the scope of your essay appropriate to the length.

8. *If you don't know what a word means, don't use it.* Even if you do know what a long word means, a short word could just as well express what you're trying to say. The SATs are your chance to flex those verbal muscles, and there is nothing worse than misusing a word.

9. *Openings are key.* Try and grab the reader's attention from the beginning. It's a different kind of writing from what you would turn in to your AP English teacher. You're telling a story, not proving that death is a major theme in *Hamlet.*

10. *Conclusions are important.* Many times, a beautifully written essay is weakened with a moral at the end of the story. Example: "And after years of hard work and perseverance, I realized that nice guys don't always finish last, that good things can come in small packages, and that when life hands you lemons, just make lemonade." Don't ruin a perfectly good essay by launching into broad, sweeping statements. If you find yourself thinking that a platitude is necessary to prove your point, start revising.

11. *Don't neglect the middle.*

12. *Be concise.* Read your essay over and over and trim unnecessary words and sentences. This is one case in which longer is not necessarily better. Try not to repeat points once made, and keep the pace of the essay flowing. Remember, your admissions officer has quite a few more essays to get through.

13. *Don't be afraid to ask for help.* Input is always good, especially since it can be hard to get perspective on your own work. Don't let your parents take away your voice from the essay, but they—or your teachers, friends, and counselors—should be able to tell you if your essay is appealing and if it accurately portrays who you are to a complete stranger.

14. *Proofread.*
15. *Proofread.*
16. *Proofread.*

Most importantly, think of these tips as guidelines. Some of them you will follow to the letter and others you may toss to the wind. Just don't say we didn't warn you.

Good luck!

MEMORABLE MOMENTS

"Sensibility"

By Amanda Davis, who attended a public high school in
Ketchikan, Alaska.

The putrid stench of rotten salmon wafts through the boardwalk, permeating the Five Star Café with a fishy odor. I stand, chopping red peppers for tomorrow's soba salad, in the back of the minuscule kitchen. Adam, a pretty boy with cropped hair, stands beside me, relating tales of snowboarding in Sweden while slicing provolone cheese. Tourists walk by the café, some peering in through the windows, others interested only in fish swimming upstream—clicks of cameras capture the endless struggle for survival. It is 3:00 in the afternoon, the lunch rush has died down, the evening rush has not yet started. I relax in the rhythmic trance of the downward motion of the knife, as I watch the red peppers fall into precise slices. The door opens. A customer.

Adam looks toward me. "Your turn."

I nod, pull myself away from the peppers, and turn to the register. A man stands, looking at me. His eyes, hidden under tangled gray hair, catch mine, and my eyes drop, down to his arms. Spider lines of old tattoos stand out, words and pictures and symbols sketched on thin, almost emaciated arms. I know I am staring. I look up.

"Can I help you?" I brightly ask.

He looks at me warily. "A cup of coffee."

Adam hands him a cup and goes back to slicing.

"That will be one dollar, sir." He fumbles in his pocket, and pulls out a wrinkled dollar bill. He extends his hand, then—suddenly— pulls back. His face changes, and he leans toward me, casting a frightened glance at the cash register.

"Is that—is that—" He stumbles over his words. "Is that alive?"

I look to the machine. Its common gray exterior rests on the counter, the green numerals displaying the amount owed. I think of my first days at the Five Star, when I was sure that it was alive—a nefarious machine manipulating the costs to cause my humiliation. As the days proceeded, we slowly gained a trust for one another, and its once evil demeanor had changed—to that of an ordinary machine. I think of the world—controlled by machines, the cars and computers and clocks— would they, could they, rise up against us? The espresso machine is behind me, it could attack—the hot water spurting forth, blinding me as the cash register falls and knocks me onto the floor as I—No, of course not.

Sensibility wins again.

"No, sir. It's just a machine," I explain. He eyes me, untrusting of my words, in need of reassurance. "It takes money." I take his dollar, and show him how, with a push of a button, I can place the money inside. He takes his coffee with both hands, and sips it.

"A machine . . ." he quietly repeats.

The cash register sits, silent on the counter.

ANALYSIS

In both subject matter and style, "Sensibility" is a breath of fresh air. Imagine reading stacks of essays about mundane topics, and then coming upon one about red peppers, provolone cheese and a cash register—how could it not stand out? Rather than describing a life-altering experience or an influential relationship, the writer reveals herself and her talents indirectly by bringing us into a captivating scene.

With the skills of a creative writer, the author uses crisp detail to make the Five Star Café spring to life and to place us in the seaside kitchen. Even if all the essay does is grab our attention and force us to remember its author, this essay is a success. But "Sensibility" has other strengths. The dialogue with the emaciated man raises provocative questions about modern life. How do we relate to the machines around us? How does "sensibility" change in this new environment? And how do machines affect our relations with people of different classes and backgrounds? The essay does not pretend to answer these questions, but in raising them it reveals its author to possess an impressive degree of sophistication and, at bottom, an interesting mind.

All the same, "Sensibility" is not without its faults. For one, the scene seems so surreal that we are led to wonder whether this is a work of fiction. An admissions essay will be stronger the more we can trust that we are hearing the author's honest, personal voice; the fictional quality here jeopardizes that. Moreover, although the author proves that she is thoughtful and talented and has a vivid imagination, many questions are left unanswered. Does the author want to be a writer? How would her creativity translate into a contribution to the community? We would need to rely on the rest of her application to fill in those gaps. Still, on the whole, "Sensibility" is successful both because of and in spite of its riskiness.

—Geoffrey C. Upton

"A Memorable Day"

By Ayana Elizabeth Johnson, who attended a small private high school in Brooklyn, New York.

Walking through meadow and forest and mud, helping and being helped across streams, looking at lakes, stars and trees, smelling pines and horses, and generally traveling through a half-seen world, all happened before four A.M. The ten of us stopped near a waterfall to absorb the beauty of the rising sun. The sky was on fire before the embers died out and only the blues and yellows remained. I saw the beams of the sun slide down from the sky and into a meadow, and felt my happiness slide down my cheeks. To the sky I sang my thanks.

As our journey to the Grand Pyramid continued, I met new flowers. At the base of its peak, I looked up with excitement, and then out for stability. Intimidated and yet determined, I started to crawl up the mountain. I found geodes, and that big rocks aren't always stable. I wasn't alone, but I was climbing by myself. At the top, the four of us who had continued from the base were greeted by the beauty of needle peaks and mountain ranges and miles of a clear view in every direction, without the bitterly cold winds and the fear of heights I had expected would be there too. There was simply nature and sunshine and friendship, and the elation they bring.

Balloons were blown up and attached to me. People danced around me and shouted, and a smile I couldn't control burst forth.

On the way down, instead of the tears of joy that had accompanied the sunrise, there were songs of joy, and I thought. I realized that the rewards and thrills and memories are in the journey and not in reaching the destination. I had believed this before and even said it out loud, but this was different. I looked at everything along the way. I stopped and rested and attempted to etch each different view into my memory. The hackneyed phrase of "enjoying every step along the way" was something I lived, and as a result I felt richer than I had ever been. I promised myself that this lesson I would never forget, but as I was descending from the highest point to which I'd ever journeyed, my thoughts too returned to a more pragmatic level. I remembered that each journey in my life wouldn't be as challenging or exciting or rewarding as this one had been; nevertheless, it is the flowers and geodes and smiles and balloons that make the journey worthwhile.

I had only been singing for myself and for the mountains, but everyone had heard me, and, when I reached the bottom, I was greeted with congratulations and laughter—after all, I did have balloons tied to me.

And the journey continued. The waterfall we had only really heard before day-break was now visible, and I was convinced to jump in and make it tangible too. I plunged my head under its torrential flow, only to receive a headache from its coldness as a reward for my boldness. I removed my-then-numbed-self from the water and was lacing up my boots when it began to hail. I had been wishing that snow would fall on this August day, but hail was close enough. The few of us who had braved the waterfall then ran to catch the group in the forest before the imminent thunderstorm arrived.

I saw in the daylight what I had (or rather hadn't) seen in the moonlight. The streams we had helped each other cross in the dark were no more than rivulets through a field in the light. The mysterious woods were turned serene by the rays of the sun, and I thought of the great chasm that often exists between appearance and reality. The mud puddles that had been obstacles were now only another detail of the landscape, and I thought about things that are a challenge to me which others find simple. The meadow where I had tripped while trying to star-gaze and walk, became a place to cloud-gaze and wonder at the storm, and I thought of the many ways different people can appreciate the same thing.

The humbling thunder approached. It growled. Suddenly, the frighteningly beautiful companion of the thunder struck a hill not so far ahead of us. A friend, the only other person who had seen it, and I ran screaming and laughing into the trees, but knew we would be all right because we were together.

A trek by moonlight, a sky on fire, leaking eyes, 13,851 feet up, balloons, geodes, songs, icy waterfalls, hail and lightning were my seventeenth birthday.

ANALYSIS

This essay is effective because it carries the metaphor of the journey of life from the climb up the mountain all the way through. The essay is well organized and structured, designed to represent the reconstruction of the author's exciting day, starting with her initial reaction to the scenery to her elation of finishing at the end. Each paragraph, though varied in length, tells a part of the journey and a change in the author's growing perspective on life.

The author uses a lot of active description, which the reader can easily relate to and almost experience a part of her journey. Phrases such as "only to receive a headache from its coldness as a reward for my boldness," speak poignantly because the reader can almost feel the sting of the dip in the waterfall. The comparison between daylight and moonlight also works well because it allows the writer a chance to demonstrate her ability to describe contrast.

The reader may be slightly disoriented by the lack of context for the story, as we are not told where the author is or why she is climbing a mountain. However, through the carefully controlled description the author reveals her reflective nature and personal realization as she ascends and descends the mountain, hence, showing the parallel physical and emotional progression. Her concluding sentence, though not particularly poignant, serves as a strong summary of a well-written piece.

—Nancy Poon

"To Freeze a Moment"

By Katya Rosenblatt, who attended a public high school in Belmont, Massachusetts, a suburb of Boston.

I rarely take pictures, and I no longer keep a regular diary. Garnering memories is a risky pastime.

Some years ago, writing in my journal used to be a customary activity. I would return from school and dedicate the expected half hour to diligently documenting the day's events, feelings, and impressions in my little blue leather-bound volume. I did not really need to vent my emotions by way of words, but I gained a certain satisfaction from seeing my experiences forever engraved on paper. After all, isn't sculpting memories a way of immortalizing the past?

When I was thirteen years old, I went hiking in Bryce Canyon, well-equipped with pens, journal, and camera. During the trip, I was obsessed with chronicling every occurrence, name and place I encountered. I felt proud to be spending my time productively, dutifully preserving for posterity a detailed account of my travels. On my last night there, I wandered out of my tent, diary in hand. The sky was illuminated by the glare of the moon, and the walls of the canyon looked menacing behind their veil of shadows. I instinctively reached for my pen . . .

At that point, I understood that nothing I wrote could ever parallel or replace the few seconds I allowed myself to experience the ineffable beauty of my surroundings. All I remembered of the previous few days were the dull characterizations I had set down in my journal. The sentences I had so tenderly molded sounded stale and bland. By stepping aside and constantly putting my adventures in perspective, I forgot to actually live them.

Now, I only write in my diary when I need to jot down a special thought or feeling. I still love to record ideas and quotations that strike me in books, or observations that are particularly meaningful. I take pictures, but not very often—only of objects I find irresistibly fascinating. I'm no longer infatuated with having something to remember when I grow old. I realize that life will simply pass me by if I stay behind the camera, too preoccupied with preserving the present so as to live it in the future.

I don't want to wake up one day and have nothing but a pile of pictures and notes. Maybe I won't have as many exact representations of people and places, maybe I'll forget certain facts, but at least the experiences will always remain inside me. I don't live to make memories—I just live, and the memories form themselves.

ANALYSIS

Rosenblatt's essay relates a moment of epiphany that has defined her life-philosophy. Although works in this genre often fall into the trap of over-shooting their bounds, waxing eloquent to the point of strained profundity, this essay safely negotiates the line between pretension and maturity. In what is always a personal statement, Rosenblatt expresses the relevance of her reflections in terms of their effect upon her self. Her conclusion remains in the first person rather than employing the dreadful "we" that seems always to degenerate into pompous preaching or universal truths.

One of this essay's greatest strengths is its readability. Rosenblatt has appropriately sized this essay for her subject matter, enabling her to hold the reader's attention throughout the piece while avoiding rambling and repetition. The opening paragraph is particularly successful in drawing us in to the narrative that she is about to present. The bold phrase "garnering memories is a risky pastime" pulls the reader through the composition by prompting him or her to ask why, a question that is not answered until later in the piece.

A striking image or a particularly unique moment would strengthen this essay. After the fourth paragraph, when she reveals her conclusion, the essay becomes a little too predictable. By taking the safe path Rosenblatt avoids the risk of a negative reaction but, at the same time, does not leave the reader asking questions, inspired to find out more. Of course, every essay is a balance between the two, and Rosenblatt's essay—though not risk-taking—offers the reader an insight into who she is.

—Alicia M. DeSantis

"Banana"

By Nathan W. Hill, who attended a small private school in
Portland, Oregon.

I was hungry and the sun impaled me on its searing ray. I wore a
wool coat, black with red cotton lining. It had served me well in the
misty foothills of the Himalayas, where His Holiness, the Dalai Lama,
gave his blessing. The coat had recently returned from a long absence.
I wore it despite the heat.

The humid weather and the final wilting blossoms of late September
conspired to fill my head with snot. The mighty hammer, Mjollnir,
pounded his lament between my ears.

I walked down to The Barn, our cafeteria, but it wouldn't open again
until three. Then, I remembered Clint, my junior year English teacher,
and walked back to the Upper School. Clint always kept a few overripe
bananas in the fruit bowl with the past due vocab tests. Laura, who
shared the office, complained of the fetid smell of rotten fruit and that
Clint made grunting noises as he worked hunched in his bow tie, over
a mound of disheveled papers. On occasion, he stretched his arm towards Laura's desk and asked her, with a bruised banana dangling
from his hand, "Would you like a banana, Laura?" With a crinkled
nose, Laura always politely replied, "No, thank you, Clint," and
watched in disgust as he wolfed it down.

The heavy wooden door to Clint's office stood propped open because
of the heat. Inside, a small electric fan sat on top of the computer; it
made an obnoxious noise between the sound of buzzing bees and
chomping teeth. A tiny strip of paper darted before the spinning blades.
Clint looked up from his work and asked with nasal condescension,
"Can I help you, Nate?"

I responded phlegmatically, "May I have a banana?" the sweat dripping off the end of my nose.

With a mixture of pity and reproach, he raised his arm to point at the wooden bowl on top of the gray file cabinet. I lifted three vocab tests away.

I grabbed it, soft and brown. Its sweet aroma distracted me from the throbbing of my head. I held the banana in my right hand, and moved my left hand to its stem, ready to divest my prey.

A thin sticky liquid started seeping through my hand. Not expecting a banana to leak, I dropped it, and heard a low thud, followed by splattering.

The banana burst open; its mushy yellow guts flew. A dripping peel remained of my search for happiness.

ANALYSIS

Hill has taken the basic narrative form in this essay and transformed it into something memorable. While Hill has alluded to the fact that he was in the Himalayas and that he was given a blessing by the Dalai Lama, he does not dwell on those events, however significant or unique. Rather, he chooses to concentrate on simple topics: hunger and a coveted banana.

The strength of Hill's essay rests with his descriptive language. The end of the essay particularly impacts the reader with vivid imagery. Few who read this essay will forget the image of an overripe banana exploding. Hill's phrasing is at times perfect: ". . . ready to divest my prey," is one such example of convincing, powerful language. Hill has conveyed the exact magnitude of his hunger and desire for that banana with this phrase.

A few areas could be strengthened, however. Hill is somewhat meandering in his opening, touching on topics like the Dalai Lama and the Himalayas, which, though interesting, are not significant to the main thrust of the narrative. Also, Hill's use of dialogue and the description of Clint and Laura are a little awkward. He might have done better to have simply expanded upon the latter paragraphs of his essay, focusing more on the banana and his hunger and omitting this dialogue and the description of Clint. Despite these small complications, Hill has done the trick and produced an essay that demands attention and respect.

—Adam S. Cohen

"A Night Unforgotten"

By Frederick Antwi, who attended Ghana International School in
Ghana, West Africa.

An hour before the commencement of the personality contest, I
deposited my bag carefully in a corner of the changing room.
From my vantage point, I could see the muscular seniors comparing
their lovely three-piece suits and musing about which one of them
would win the title. A bony, stuttering junior with no suit and no new
shoes, I swallowed hard and resolved to give the pageant my best shot.
Since the first round of the program was a parade in traditional wear,
I nervously pulled out my kente, draped the beautifully woven red and
yellow fabric around my thin frame, pinned on my "contestant number
five" badge and hurried to take my place in line.

Wishing hopelessly that my mother was among the spectators and
not working in some hospital in a foreign country, I stepped out onto
the polished wooden stage. Immediately, one thousand two hundred
curious eyes bore into me. My cheeks twitched violently, my throat
constricted and my knees turned to jelly. I fought for control. Bending
my arms slightly at the elbows, I strutted across the stage in the usual
fashion of an Asante monarch and mercifully made it back to the
changing room without mishap. The crowd erupted into a frenzied
cheer. As I returned for the "casual wear" round, something magical
happened.

It was a singular emotion that no words can describe. It began as
an aching, beautiful tenderness in the pit of my stomach, gradually
bubbling into my chest, filling me with warmth and radiance, melting
away all the tension. Slowly, it effervesced into my mouth, onto my
tongue and into words. As I spoke to the crowd of my pastimes and
passions, words of such silky texture poured out from my soul with
unparalleled candor and cadence. The voice that issued from my lips

was at once richer, deeper, stronger than I had ever produced. It was as though an inner self, a core essence, had broken free and taken control. Severed from reality, I floated through the remainder of that remarkable evening.

One hour later, the baritone of the presenter rang out into the cool night air. "Mr. GIS Personality 1993, selected on the basis of confidence, charisma, cultural reflection, style, eloquence, wit and originality, is Contestant number . . ."

"Five! One! Five! Five!" roared the electrified crowd.

My heart pounded furiously. My breathing reduced to shallow gasps.

"Contestant number five!" exploded the presenter in confirmation.

For a few sacred moments, time stopped. My ears screamed, and my lower jaw, defying the grip of my facial muscles, dropped like a draw-bridge. Then I rushed forward, bear-hugged the presenter and embraced everyone else I could lay my hands on! Amidst the tumult, the Manager of KLM Airlines mounted the stage, presenting me with a meter-long Accra-Amsterdam-London return ticket. As I stood brandishing my sky-blue cardboard ticket, posing shamelessly for the cameras and grinning sheepishly at the throng, a pang of regret shot through me. If only my mother could have been in that crowd to witness and indeed be a part of this most poignant of all memories.

ANALYSIS

"The unusual experience" is a staple of college entrance essays, but in this case the experience is truly unusual—a personality contest for men? It's also interesting to see Antwi's transformation from shy to superstar. Antwi concentrates on a fixed event in time and uses it to show the spectrum of his personality—shy, confident, excited, lonely—in an amusing and entertaining way.

It's no wonder Antwi won the contest. He's a great storyteller. He has an acute sense of detail—"one thousand two hundred curious eyes," "the fashion of an Asante monarch"—and is good at heightening drama. The essay is also upbeat and fun to read.

It would have been nice to know what Antwi said in the third paragraph instead of simply reading about the "unparalleled candor and cadence" with which he spoke. Also, Antwi does not explain the what, where, or why of the contest, which are all important to know. Overall, however, his personality shines through as stellar.

—Caille M. Millner

"A Lesson about Life"

By Aaron Miller, who attended a large public school in
Aptos, California.

Finally the day had arrived. I was on my way to Aspen, Colorado.
I had heard wonderful stories about the Aspen Music School from
friends who had attended in previous years, and I was certain that this
summer would be an unbelievable learning experience. I was especially excited to be studying with Mr. Herbert Stessin, an esteemed
professor from the Juilliard School.

After just a few lessons with Mr. Stessin, I knew that I would not
be disappointed. Mr. Stessin is so incredibly sharp that no detail gets
by him. He notices every turn of each musical phrase, catches wrong
notes in complex chords, and interjects his wry sense of humor into
every lesson. As I was preparing Beethoven's Sonata, Op. 31, No. 3,
for a master class, he warned me at the end of a lesson, "Don't play
this too well, Aaron, or I'll have nothing to say!"

The master class went quite well considering that it was my first
performance of the sonata. A few days later, as I walked across the
bridge over the creek which winds through the music school campus,
I saw Mr. Stessin's wife, Nancy, who was also on the Aspen faculty.
I waved to her, and as I walked past she said something to me which I
didn't catch over the roar of the rushing water. I stopped for a moment
as she repeated, "That was a very nice Beethoven you played the other
day." We had a brief conversation, and I was touched by her thoughtful
comment.

On July 15 I had my last lesson with Mr. Stessin, and walked
with him to the dining hall. As I was sitting down with my friends to
have lunch, someone whispered to me, "Mrs. Stessin passed out!"
We naturally assumed that she had fainted from the altitude or the
heat. However, we soon realized that the situation was more serious,

as an ambulance was called to take her to the nearby hospital.

Nothing could have prepared me for the news that two distraught friends brought late that night to my roommate and me. Mrs. Stessin had never regained consciousness and had died of a ruptured aneurysm. That night, my roommate and I could not sleep; we talked about our memories of Mrs. Stessin for hours on end. In the morning, Dean Laster called us together to officially announce the sad news.

Numb with disbelief that this vibrant and dedicated woman was gone, we wondered how Mr. Stessin could possibly cope with this terrible tragedy. Surely he would be heading back to New York as soon as arrangements could be made.

I couldn't have been more wrong. Only days later, Mr. Stessin was back in his studio, teaching!

Initially shocked by Mr. Stessin's decision to stay, I soon began to understand his thinking. He and his wife had been teaching at Aspen for many years and had built a strong sense of community with the faculty and students. Furthermore, I realized that he found comfort through his love of music and his commitment to his students. Leaving Aspen would have meant leaving behind his fondest memories of Nancy.

After studying a Mozart piano concerto with Mr. Stessin all summer, I was fortunate to win the Nakamichi Piano Concerto competition, but even more fortunate to have the opportunity to dedicate my performance to the memory of Mrs. Stessin. At the end of the concert, my last evening in Aspen, I was greeted by friends and faculty members backstage. When I saw Mr. Stessin approaching me, he was beaming. "That was a wonderful performance!" he said, and gave me a hug. He continued, "And thank you for the dedication. I'll miss you." We hugged again.

Last summer did indeed turn out to be an unbelievable learning experience. Although Mr. Stessin taught me a great deal about music and the piano, in the end his greatest lesson was about life.

ANALYSIS

Miller builds a strong essay around two big stories: a phenomenal accomplishment and a moving death.

He has a good ear for coupling dialogue and narration, and projects himself with attractive modesty. Miller offers the reader a chance to appreciate an especially wide range of qualities: empathy, virtuosity, wisdom, and generosity, although he misses a good opportunity to describe how he feels about the music he performs, and his conclusion is somewhat trite.

Miller limits his essay to a scope that makes sense. Relating a personal tragedy can be key to allowing the reader to appreciate one's maturity, but one must have a gentle touch and healthy emotional distance.

—Matthew A. Carter

"Running Thoughts"

By Nikhil Kacker, who attended a small suburban public high school in Northbrook, Illinois.

I closed my eyes and slowly took a deep breath. The gun rang loudly in my ears as the runners sprinted out of the start, pushing and shoving for the lead. I ran out with a fast, long stride, trying to keep my breathing even, while counting my strides in my head. I threw elbows to my left and right as we jostled for position. As the lead group turned the first corner, I lost count when my leg hit a cone on the course. Veering towards the outside, I cut someone off behind me and heard a yell of protest. Suddenly, I was flying towards the ground.

My hands scraped the gravel on my way down, stinging with pain. Someone had tripped me! Quickly, I pushed myself up from the dirt and sprinted back to the lead, heart pounding frantically in my chest. That was a stupid move; I almost cost the race for the whole team. I suddenly felt weak; instead of running, I was dragging my body.

As I plodded on, thoughts of marching band practice later in the day brought our show abruptly into my head. I began running to the beat of "Robin Hood." I found strength and energy flow into my body. My limbs suddenly seemed lighter and more flexible, ready to be pushed even further.

"Nikhil, let's keep moving. Keep the pace up!" shouted my coach from the mile mark. I started pumping my arms harder, propelling myself faster. Widening the gap between the other runners and myself, I fell into a rhythm. Everything seems to be in harmony, just like Lao-Tzu believed. I suddenly thought of the history paper I had to write on Taoism this weekend. It was going to take so long that I doubted I would be able to go out with friends tonight. My shoulders began to tighten and I felt my lungs turn to lead.

Thump, thump. I glanced behind and saw a runner within twenty feet of me. My heart skipped a beat while I raced ahead and increased my lead. Reaching the gravel pavement, my spiked shoes created a pulsating crackle on the hard rocks. The grating roar of pebbles which the waves suck back and fling at their return. Sitting on the pebble beach in Nice with friends, laughing and joking. The warm sun enveloped me. A smile spread across my face.

The roar of the crowd near the finish sent renewed energy into my exhausted legs. Turning the last corner, my mind went blank; all I felt was a force pushing me towards the end, causing me to sprint faster and faster. Crossing the line, I collapsed in the grass, heaving and panting. I had won, I had won. That's all that went through my mind. As I struggled to catch my breath, I reminded myself, as after every race: "Each race is a drama, a challenge. Each race stretches me one way and another and each race tells me more about myself and others."

ANALYSIS

This essay effectively combines the details of a specific event in the author's high school career as well as her general interests and experiences. The reader learns that the writer not only enjoys competitive track but that she likes marching band, studying history, and traveling. We learn that the writer is multidimensional and get a glimpse of how she balances all these interests. Small details, such as hearing the sounds of "Robin Hood," are integrated so that the essay is not simply a list of her extracurricular activities, but actually a look inside the mind of the writer captured in those few minutes of the race.

The overall tone of the essay is effective in conveying the excitement of the race, but the writer is also careful to break the monotone of describing that one event with the constant shift back to her mental thoughts on the other aspects of her life. This is also reflected in the variation of sentence structure, which helps keep the reader's attention.

Although we do learn a lot about the writer's interests in this essay, discussing more about why she enjoys them is a possible area of improvement. In addition, while the concluding quote ties in the story nicely, citing a quote at the end of an essay often results in the loss of the personal voice of the writer and should be considered carefully.

—Nancy Poon

"Playing the Giramel's Behind"

By Eliot I. Hodges, who attended a small private high school in
Washington, D.C.

In the Washington Opera's production of Mozart's "The Magic
Flute," Tamino, the Singsmiel's protagonist, charms fantastic, hy-
brid animals such as the Pantelot, the Ostremu, and the Chimpaboon
into following him by playing a mellifluous melody on his magical flute.
If you have had the opportunity to enjoy this opera at the Kennedy
Center, then you must have also seen a nine-foot tall concoction of a
giraffe and a camel known as a Giramel waddling among its fellow
fauna. I played its posterior.

As the Giramel's behind, not much of me was to be seen, since my
legs, which were dressed in Pepto-Bismol—colored tights, and my feet,
masqueraded as gigantic, cartoon-like hooves, were my only visible
parts—the rest was neatly tucked into the vast wire-and-foam interior
of the pink behemoth. As sprightly as the Giramel might have appeared
on stage, it demanded considerable doing on my part to help animate
the animal, be it through a shuffle of hoof, a shake of hip, or a swirl of
tail. I needed a lot of practice.

Two months to be exact, but when using a "practice/real-time con-
version scale," this translates into five minutes of real stage time per
performance. There were eleven performances.

Despite being a supernumerary, the pawn of the opera hierarchy, I
had a passion for bringing the Giramel's derrière to life. This was partly
due to my recall of Sherlock Holmes' words: "It has long been an axiom
of mine that the little things are infinitely the most important." This,
of course, is an obvious overstatement of my position as the invisible
puppeteer of the Giramel's nether set of cheeks, but it helped explain
a sentiment I have about the arts: be it a mere street-crosser in a
spaghetti Western or a triangle's chime in a symphony, everything is

of inherent value to the finished product—provided, of course, that it is done well.

Thus, I saw my Giramel career as being much like one of the specks in Jackson Pollack's "No. 9"—almost undiscernible when standing alone, but of value when seen as a part of the whole.

ANALYSIS

This essay, an example of a unique personal experience, mixes humor and culture to form a lethal one-two punch. Appearing on the Kennedy Center stage is something of which to be proud, even if it is as the rump of an imaginary animal. Hodges does well to show who he is—he has a sense of humor, he is a good writer and he is obviously a talented performer. (Do you realize how hard it would be to shake *that* booty?)

It is not uncommon for a college applicant to write about his role as the lead in a high school, community, or even professional performance and how much he learned from it. Hodges has set himself apart from these people in the first paragraph by admitting to something most would want to forget about. True, he does go on to tell how valuable an experience it was, but *anyone* would learn from that experience—at the very least a lesson in humility. Humility is probably the best character trait to write about. It lets you talk about yourself without being too cocky.

Hodges's essay is not perfect, however. Despite his writing talent, his sentences tend to be long and brimming with clauses. The admissions officer who reads the essay will likely have been reading essays all day. While Hodges has set himself apart, long sentences can turn the reader off fast. You are not going to prove that you are the next Dickens in fewer than 500 words. On the flip side, if you tend too much toward Hemingway, you might want to beef up your writing with some color. Description is good, but not to the point where it slows down the pace of the essay.

—William P. Bohlen

"A Competitive Friendship"

By Justin Barkley, who attended a large public high school in suburban Birmingham, Alabama.

I firmly believe competition can be a good thing—so long as it motivates us to succeed and to understand that what is truly important is not grades or standardized test scores; but rather learning new things and doing one's best. It is good for one to outperform his friends, so long as they remain his friends. An example of this kind of healthy, friendly competition exists between my best friend, Warren Carroll, and me.

Warren and I compete for everything: having the highest grades, being the best dressed, even flirting with the prettiest girls. We were both nominated Most Likely to Succeed by our graduating class, an honor which Warren won. And we both ran for vice-president of National Honor Society, an office which I now hold. We are both National Merit Semifinalists and are both in the top ten of our class. However, our fiercest competition has been for achieving the highest standardized test scores.

First came the SAT. Warren got a 1510, and I got a 1540. We both decided to take the test again to try to get a perfect 1600 score. My score dropped to 1530 while his rose to 1550! I reluctantly ceded the "King of the SAT" crown to Warren.

Then came the ACT. Warren threw down the gauntlet by taking it first and getting a 35. He decided that was a good enough score and did not take it again. When it came my turn to take the exam, I asked Warren for a few pointers. He recommended some practice exam books, but I never really used them. Imagine my surprise then when I learned that I had aced the ACT with a perfect 36! Warren genuflected before the "King of the ACT."

Now, it turns out that scoring 36 on every one of the four subsections of the ACT is a rare, even newsworthy event. I had a front page article written about me in the *Birmingham News*. The story was then sent over the wires and picked up by newspapers all across Alabama. I was interviewed on the radio by WERC's morning team, Doug and John Ed. I was even interviewed on television with WBRC's Janice Rogers on her morning show, "Good Day, Alabama."

Television cameras even invaded our school as Channel 6 wanted to video me in the courtyard with some friends for their evening newscast. At first, the camera man told us to stand there and talk as though he was not there. It was very awkward at first, trying to act casual with a TV camera in my face and my friends trying to make me laugh. Warren was the only person who tried to act normally, and he asked me about a calculus test we had had earlier that day. Then, the camera man said he wanted a shot of all of us together as though we were posing for a photograph. Girls actually began fighting to stand next to me. Class President Ross Litkenhous' girlfriend, Melissa Barberini, pushed her way to my right side, and Abbey McGough stood at my left until she was pushed aside by Kim Griffin, a girl whom Warren and I have often competed for attention. As the picture was being taken I looked at Warren. He had only scored one point lower than I had scored on the ACT, yet I was being filmed for TV with my arm around Kim. He had more reason than anyone to be jealous, yet he was the one person trying to be supportive. That night I called Warren to thank him for being such a great friend.

While I still get recognized occasionally by total strangers as that kid that got a 36 on the ACT and girls (like cheerleader Tamsyn Morgan and dance team member Nicole Clemons) who never talked to me before I became a minor local celebrity still stop by my locker to say hello, the frenzied excitement that followed my perfect score is pretty much over. Through it all, Warren never showed the slightest sign of jealousy. A friend like him may be more rare than a perfect ACT score, although unfortunately not as newsworthy, it seems. Warren and I joke about taking the ACT or SAT again, to settle this matter once and for all, but we have affirmed that a great friendship like ours is more important than any competition. Although, he was getting a little flirty with Kim today in calculus . . .

ANALYSIS

Perhaps more than any other part of an admissions application, the essay offers an applicant a chance to truly "market" him or herself as a candidate who stands out from the crowd. While the writer should work to highlight his or her strong points, doing so requires special care not to come across as too arrogant or pretentious. In the case above, the author takes on a very tricky task—writing about his impressive standardized test scores. But by detailing his achievements in the context of competition between best friends, the author works to make light of his extraordinary academic performance. With a witty ending, he illustrates the supreme importance of good friendship in his life—something that is surely appealing to the sympathetic reader.

The author creates a nice sense of balance at the beginning of his essay by contrasting the ways he and his best friend had competed in high school. With a light and jovial tone, he encourages the reader to discover what continued to drive the intense competition between the two friends. By admitting his "defeat" in SAT scores, the reader sees that the author approaches test-taking with a balanced outlook, much like he creates in his essay. By the same token, the author deftly succeeds at making the actual test scores a non-issue. Instead, he does a good job at making their interplay a case of light-hearted "one-upmanship." Finally, by painting a clear picture of the frenzied atmosphere caused by his perfect ACT scores, the author provides a good contrast for the way in which his friend proves himself to be the best friend he really is.

While on the whole the author does a good job at tempering his academic successes for the reader's benefit, he does lose sight of this goal from time to time. Although there is merit in clarifying the significance of a perfect ACT score, doing so will win the author less respect with an admissions officer who may already have a list of his test scores on paper. Instead a tactful mention of the score might garner more respect for its display of modesty. That in mind, before including gratuitous scores or grades in an essay, the author should evaluate whether the mention of the specific figure adds anything to the essay.

—Scott A. Resnick

"Checkmate"

By Robert M. Stolper, who attended a public high school in
New City, New York.

Sword in hand, the black knight leapt forward and in one mighty
swing fell the king's loyal guard. The king backed away, a feeling
of helplessness washing over him. Suddenly, one of the knight's hench-
men, spiked mace in hand, appeared behind the king, trapping the
ruler. Nowhere to go. Nothing to do. The king knew it was over.

I pushed the chess piece over in disgust. Another game, another
loss. This was becoming monotonous. I played chess with my grandfather maybe once a month. And almost every time I lost. He knew
the moves and maneuvers, the counters and the attacks. But most of
all, he knew me. "Good game, Robby," my grandfather said. He stood,
fixed his silk shirt and Brooks Brothers tie, and winked. "You had a
couple of good moves, but you've got to keep thinking." He gave me
a hug. "Good game."

Whenever we're together, my grandfather and I always seem to end
up playing chess. We usually play late into the night, listening to
classical music and discussing world events. I can remember one particular night, when we played until three-thirty in the morning.

It was like any other game. Each move took my grandfather three
or four minutes. He carefully planned each action, contemplated every
possible countermaneuver, and then double checked to see if he forgot
any conceivable move. That is why he's so difficult to beat. And why
he's so difficult to play. He thinks like he plays: careful, deliberate,
and precise. It's taken me a while to understand him. In fact, it's taken
me a while to understand myself. Not everything can be seen as easily
as in chess. Not all moves are as predictable; not all decisions are as
defined. As I look back on the games I've played with my grandfather,
I wonder if he knows how much he's really taught me. That patience

is learned; that concentration is developed; that persistence pays off in the end. I wonder if I should tell him.

We sat down for yet another game of chess. At first, the battle went poorly for me. My forces were in retreat, and I had to sacrifice piece after piece to protect my king. Down went my bishop, down went my rook, down went my queen. But I slowed the pace of the game, and changed retreat to advance. I contemplated each move, and after a while I had his king surrounded. Then, in a surprise maneuver, his king took my knight. "Nice move, Grandpa," I said as I slid my rook forward. "Checkmate."

He taught me more than he knew. "Good game, Robby. Good game."

ANALYSIS

This essay demonstrates how one specific event or moment in a person's daily life can be used to reflect the character and inner workings of the author. This type of essay is frequently used and, if done properly, can show what is really important to the applicant. Whether it be playing an instrument in the school orchestra, playing tennis on your varsity team, or playing chess with your grandfather, an essay describing the feelings surrounding the action is what counts. An essay in this genre gives the author a chance to give a more personal and emotional feeling to the admissions application.

The strength in this essay is its simplicity. Stolper creatively introduces the relationship between himself and his grandfather through a common interest—chess. We can see that Stolper enjoys his time with his grandfather and the challenge to improve his own game. The introduction is especially intriguing. We don't initially know what to expect or what the essay is about. The detailed illustration of the king's futile situation is much more exciting than if Stolper had simply told us he was playing chess. As the essay progresses, the relationship further unfolds. The use of dialogue allows the reader to envision the two characters playing the game. By the end, we want and expect Stolper to win. This essay is truly enjoyable to read. It is the simplicity of the characters as well as the story that make it work.

One area for improvement might be the casual mention of personal improvement near the end of the essay. In the fourth paragraph, Stolper writes, "It's taken me a while to understand myself." Unfortunately, there is no development of this point. How has he come to understand himself and what has he learned? Although an explanation might distract the reader from the focus of the essay, the reader is more concerned with the development of the grandson.

—Daniel A. Shapiro

INFLUENCES

"Dandelion Dreams"

By Emmeline Chuang, who attended a large public high school in
New York City.

My big sister once told me that if I shut my eyes and blew on a dandelion puff, all of my wishes would come true. I used to believe her and would wake up early in the morning to go dandelion hunting. How my parents must have laughed to see me scrambling out in the backyard, plucking little gray weeds, and blowing out the seeds until my cheeks hurt.

I made the most outrageous wishes. I wished to own a monkey, a parrot, and a unicorn; I wished to grow up and be just like She-Ra, Princess of Power. And, of course, I wished for a thousand more wishes so I would never run out.

I always believed my wishes would come true. When they didn't, I ran to my sister and demanded an explanation. She laughed and said I just hadn't done it right.

"It only works if you do it a certain way," she told me with a little smile. I watched her with wide, admiring eyes and thought she must be right. She was ten years older than me and knew the ways of the world; nothing she said could be wrong. I went back and tried again.

Time passed, and I grew older. My "perfect" sister left home—not telling my parents where she had gone. Shocked by her apparent fall from grace, I spent most of my time staring out the window. I wondered where she had gone and why she hadn't told us where she was going. Occasionally, I wandered outside to pluck a few dandelions and wish for my sister's return. Each time, I hoped desperately that I had done it the right way and that the wish would come true.

But it never happened.

After a while, I gave up—not only on my sister—but on the dandelions as well. Shock had changed to anger and then to rejection of my sister and everything she had told me. The old dreamer within me vanished and was replaced by a harsh teen-age cynic who told me over and over that I should have known better than to believe in free wishes. It chided me for my past belief in unicorns and laughed at the thought of my growing up to be a five foot eleven, sleek She-Ra. It told me to stop being silly and sentimental and to realize the facts of life, to accept what I was and what my sister was, and live with it.

For a while I tried. I abandoned my old dreams, my old ideas, and threw myself entirely into school and the whole dreary rat race of scrabbling for grades and popularity. After a time, I even began to come out ahead and could start each day with an indifferent shrug instead of a defeated whimper. Yet none of it made me happy. For some reason, I kept on thinking about dandelions and my sister.

I tried to forget about both, but the edge of my anger and disillusionment wore away and the essence of my old self started to seep through again. Despite the best efforts of the cynic in me, I continually found myself staring out at those dandelions—and making wishes.

It wasn't the same as before, of course. Most of my old dreams and ideals had vanished forever. Certainly, I could never wish for a unicorn as a pet and actually mean it now. No, my dreams were different now, less based on fantasy and more on reality.

Dreams of becoming a princess in a castle or a magical sorceress had changed into hopes of someday living in the woods and writing novels like J. D. Salinger, or playing Tchaikovsky's Concerto in A to orchestral accompaniment. These were the dreams that floated through my mind now. They were tempered by a caution that hadn't been there before, but they were there. For the first time since my sister's departure, I was acknowledging their presence.

I had to, for it was these dreams that diluted the pure meaninglessness of my daily struggles in school and made me happy. It was these dreams and the hope of someday fulfilling them that ultimately saved me from falling into the clutches of the dreaded beast of apathy that lurked alongside the trails of the rat race. Without them, I think I would have given up and stumbled off the tracks long ago.

It took a long time for me to accept this truth and to admit that my cynical self was wrong in denying me my dreams, just as my youthful self had been wrong in living entirely within them. In order to succeed and survive, I needed to find a balance between the two.

My sister was right; I hadn't been going after my dreams the right way. Now I know better. This time around, when I go into the garden and pick my dandelion puff, my wishes will come true.

ANALYSIS

This essay works by portraying the immense effect of a single experience upon the life of the author. The writer's strength lies not in her language or her rhetoric, but in the narrative that she tells. It is the experience itself that actually makes this essay successful. The story is indeed a compelling one and the reader leaves the page with a desire to know more about Chuang.

The beginning of the essay works especially well in slowly captivating the reader. The opening is strong. Though it could be taken as artificial, the vivid image of the girl in the dandelions nevertheless grabs our attention. The steady progression of the narrative climaxes in the sixth paragraph, as the pointedly bold statement "but it never happened" takes the reader by surprise. At this moment, the reader is fully engaged in Chuang's narrative.

In fact, the reader is so drawn in by Chuang's story that the essay's rambling in the second half is frustrating. Perhaps this problem could have been alleviated had the author spent more time elaborating upon a specific moment in her struggle with this experience.

In the end, the sincerity at the heart of the narrative is very redeeming. The very tone of the narrative expresses a great deal about the author. Ultimately, Chuang is not merely a name at the top of the page, but a real person, with a real experience that an admissions officer can remember.

—Alicia M. DeSantis

"The Watch"

Roman Altshuler, who attended a midsized public high school in Providence, Rhode Island.

I look around me and the room has changed imperceptibly and over-tly. There are elephants on thin legs lining the walls, the people around me have become giant insects, my watch melts and slowly drips from my wrist. A Dalinian dream? A Kafkaesque nightmare? The breeze of surrealism blows through my hair; an existential whirlwind captures my imagination.

In the images of these two great creators, I see reflections of beau-tiful and insatiable imaginations, completely undisciplined, un-bounded; yet full of the magic and power of the artists' visions. These images are not as true as photographs, but they are a hundred times more honest. I, too, often find myself misrepresenting the world. In the midst of a truly dreary lecture I sometimes force wakefulness upon myself by images of what I am learning, and instead of seeing my teacher carrying on about the military campaigns of the Civil War, I see muskets blazing against raised flags.

More often, I see my life as an adventure; romanticized, idealized, exhilarating. Instead of seeing a boring test of memory, I see a test of will; instead of a debate, I see a battle of wits; instead of seeing the photographic image of life, I see the existential and intoxicating war of man against Fate itself. In these images I am sometimes challenged by faceless opponents, sometimes I am climbing a mountain. Perhaps I am fighting a bull or jumping on rooftops.

At times I question the benefits of reinventing the world to suit my fancy. It is true, of course, that everyone does this. Even the strictest of thinkers cannot avoid letting their own vision of the world show through in their works. Dali and Kafka are not exceptions, they are extremes. Why are we all so eager to get away from reality? I find that I, like many others, often don't seem to fully belong. But of course I do belong, this is my world as much as anyone else's. I try to solve this contradiction between the perceived and the real by altering the world ever so slightly—a horse-drawn carriage instead of a car, a prize-winning essay rather than another homework assignment—so that it finds its place around me.

A simple solution indeed. We do not change ourselves to fit the world, but change the world to fit within us. A simple act of wish fulfillment, and all is done. And, of course, to melt a watch with the mind is far better than to enslave the intellect within the watch like a genie in a bottle. Freedom to think requires only so little, and to adjust the world to one's thought is ever more noble than adjusting thought to the world.

ANALYSIS

This is a very good essay: short, simple, to the point. An interesting idea is introduced, discussed, neatly resolved. Roman makes nice use of structure and language: the words he uses are appropriate, and he clearly feels comfortable using them. (Too many college essays read as if they were written with thesaurus in hand. This is a welcome example of how complicated language can sound sophisticated without sounding aspiring or pretentious. Clearly, Roman has read his share of good French philosophy.)

Another strong feature of this essay is that it is distinctly personal without explicitly trying to be so. Although it is brief—barely 500 words—the reader comes out with a clear impression of the author's personality, his basic philosophy, and his take on life. His clear presentation of thoughts imply that these are simply a few in an ongoing internal dialogue; the essay serves as a passing glance into the current state of Roman's mind. And it is an engaging, original, and provocative mind. This essay, as any discussion of thoughts, is quite revealing; it would be a good balance to the factual, numerical information provided on the rest of the college application.

Notice that these are all Roman's thoughts. While it's evident that he's read and synthesized a lot of ideas, he doesn't directly quote anyone here, nor try to impress the reader by dropping names. Kafka and Dali come naturally; it is evident that he has a good command of their genres, and didn't just mention people he found in the dictionary of quotations.

My criticisms are not glaring, and serve more as suggestions for another draft than imperatives for the current one. First, as the average college essay is 500–800 words, there is room for another paragraph; if written as tightly as the ones above, it wouldn't be extraneous, and could only add. Second, this essay does raise questions as to the danger of overtly subjective thought. While this isn't the place to raise and solve a great philosophical question, summary treatment of reality (or a line about how "seeing" things differently gives the author the perspective to take the real world at face value) might be nice. The reader might be happier if put somewhere back in the status quo, rather than left suspended in theoretical ether.

—Maryanthe Malliaris

"A Great Influence"

By Michelangelo V. D'Agostino, who attended a small Catholic school in Chicago, Illinois.

Albert Einstein must have been a truly quirky individual. Though a patent officer by day, he worked into the wee hours of the morning on his revolutionary theories. I can just see him with his mass of white hair splayed out on his desk catching up on some long-overdue sleep. Of all the science teachers that I have ever had, only one has been comparable to Albert Einstein; only one has been able to truly appreciate physics like Einstein and been able to instill this deep appreciation in others.

Mr. Michael Peterson walked into the classroom for the first day of A.P Physics flouting the standard notions of a teacher at St. Ignatius. He wore khaki shorts, an open-necked golf shirt, and deck shoes with no socks. The most striking features of his appearance were the two dark blue semi-circles underneath his eyes. He appeared to be somewhere between a raccoon and a test subject for a psychological experiment on sleep deprivation. He was always to be found holding a mug of caffeinated beverage, whether it be Pepsi, Jolt, or Mountain Dew. He went on to inform us that he did not sleep much (as if we couldn't already tell), between teaching and working on his own theories. Like Einstein, he loved what he was doing, and he spent as much time as possible pursuing his goals.

His method of teaching was also unlike any I had previously experienced. He emphasized pragmatism and creativity through hands-on projects and creative writing assignments. One of the major projects that we pursued was the building of a go-cart. For three weeks we hammered and greased our way into a better understanding of what we were studying. One of the major problems we encountered was with the brake system: we just couldn't figure out how to make it work. With a wry smile on his face, Mr. Peterson said, "I would advise that you figure it out. Brakes are a pretty important part of a car." He taught us that the answer will not always be in a book. There will not always be a teacher to swoop down like a guardian angel with all the answers. We successfully worked out the problem ourselves, and our brakes were able to stop on a dime. Okay, maybe a quarter. Einstein once said that knowledge is nothing without imagination. Mr. Peterson truly comprehended this ideal and stood behind it.

Obviously his methods worked. People were interested in science, and grades reflected it. We all looked forward to coming to class every day. The administration did not appreciate his efforts though. He was told that he must either teach from the text in a more orthodox manner, or he must leave. He said that it would be unfair to sell his students down the river. Consequently, he lost his job.

Towards the end of the year, Mr. Peterson faced his uncertain future with composure. He said that for all he knew he might be flipping greasy hamburgers this time next year, but he didn't mind. If Albert Einstein was a patent officer, why couldn't a fast-food worker revolutionize science? Someday Mr. Michael Peterson could be receiving the Nobel Prize for physics. And you know what? I wouldn't be the least bit surprised. He taught me to love science, to value creativity, and to be true to my ideals. In this way he has forever influenced my life.

ANALYSIS

The essay highlights aspects of the author's personality via an examination of how that personality has been affected by another individual, in this case, an unorthodox schoolteacher. The essay proceeds by describing this teacher, and his interaction with the author, concluding with a description of how that interaction has imparted upon the author a series of important lessons in both science and in life.

What makes the essay work is its strong sense of organization. The reader is taken smoothly from the enticing introduction, through the description of the author's teacher, to the eventual conclusion of the teacher being fired and the author's reflection on the teacher's influence. The essay's use of analogies and similarities is also effective. The description of the teacher's independent work in physics strengthens the reader's appreciation for the lessons of independent thought and problem-solving that seem to be imparted upon the author through his classroom experiences. The analogy between the author's teacher and famous theoretical physicist Albert Einstein also showcases the author's appreciation for another one of life's ironic lessons—that sometimes the most brilliant minds and teachers are also the most unorthodox and misunderstood ones.

The essay could be improved, however, by giving us a better background on the author's views and ideals prior to his interaction with the physics teacher. Although the reader is given a clear view of what lessons the author has learned via this interaction, it is not clear as to how much of a transformation has truly occurred in the author's character. By describing the author's character prior to his experiences with the teacher, the essay could serve to better position these experiences within the course of the author's development.

—Elliot Shmukler

"Michael and Me"

Name withheld for privacy

Michael is my best friend. I would trust him with my life. We have known each other and attended the same schools since first grade. We played on Little League and basketball teams together, and we lifted weights at his house every day after school. Our relationship was the epitome of male bonding.

Michael has significantly influenced the person I have become. In school he strives for excellence and achieves it. He has a unique ability to relate to people. He is committed, driven and self-confident. Emotionally, he is the strongest person I know. These are qualities that I also see in myself. Just as I appreciate Michael's qualities, he appreciates mine; when I asked Michael for three words to describe me, his answers were "loyal, driven and optimistic." I am committed to giving respect to those who are entitled to it, such as my parents, teachers and coaches. My friends and teammates are extremely important to me. My drive, self-confidence and willingness to chance failure have allowed me to take on challenges others might not consider. These challenges define my life by constantly providing inspiration. I try to live my life according to a Japanese proverb: "Fall seven times, stand up eight." Lastly, I have always been an optimist, and I love to laugh. My friends and family marvel at my jovial nature. Many times my family had considered placing me on a respirator after hearing me erupt in laughter at a Dave Barry book or an episode of "The Simpsons."

Last year, Michael told me he was gay. I was dumbfounded. Looking back, I realized that I had failed to notice emerging signs of his sexuality. I wondered how I, his best friend, could have failed to see them. Friends had approached me and asked if Michael was gay. My answer was always, "Of course not!" Then I realized why his revelation came as a shock. My closest friends are those that I not only admire but emulate. Michael has played a major part in shaping my personality. In fact, our friends often comment that we "share a brain." I never considered that he might be gay because I knew I was not.

I soon found that I had no problem with Michael's sexuality. I realized that he had helped me to reject prejudices and accept people for who they are. "Coming out of the closet" was an ordeal for Michael, and it took every ounce of his emotional strength to deal with it. While he always told himself that I knew him better than anyone else and that he could tell me anything, he hid himself from me. Now that I know, our relationship has become stronger, and we know that nothing will ever come between us.

His courage inspired me to participate in the September 1997 Boston–New York AIDS Ride 3. I did not even have a bicycle, and raising the funds, training and finishing this 275-mile ride through the hills of New England was the toughest challenge I have faced in my life, but I did it with a new awareness.

Michael is still the same person I love and admire. His revelation did not change him—it changed me.

ANALYSIS

In this essay, the author tackles a controversial subject—homosexuality—in an honest and humane way. Through describing his close friendship, he reveals himself to be a compassionate and loyal person, open to new perspectives and willing to adapt to and learn about the needs and feelings of those around him.

The essay has two main strengths: its clear narrative structure and its direct, confident writing style. The author tells the story of his friendship with Michael without trying to add complexity to the issues involved. He starts by explaining what their friendship means to him; recounts the most significant moment in the friendship and how he dealt with it, and concludes with how his friendship has become stronger as a result. It is not a new story, but that it is told without pretense makes it fresh and readable, and makes us like its author. The vocabulary is not highfalutin and the sentence structure is as simple as can be. As a result, the author appears genuine and nothing gets in the way of the emotions being expressed.

Of course, the essay could be improved. For one, the author could have added a good bit more detail about his friendship with Michael without compromising the simple and direct style. Instead, many sentences are too general to have a lasting impact on the reader and sound a bit clichéd (e.g. "Our relationship has become stronger, and we know that nothing will ever come between us.") More curiously, the author spends too many words in the second paragraph describing and, indeed, praising his own personality. Though he starts off the paragraph well, explaining what he and Michael had in common, we are left to wonder what the extensive self-description adds to the story of his friendship. In total, however, the essay is a winner precisely because of its overall honesty and its prevailing lesson of selflessness.

—Geoffrey C. Upton

"A Mixture"

By Anjanette Marie Chan Tack, who attended a small public school in
Pointe-a-Pierre, Trinidad and Tobago.

They will send the Indians to India,
Send the Africans to Africa,
Well, somebody please just tell me
Where they're sending poor me, poor me?
Because I'm neither one or the other,
Six of one, half a dozen of the other,
I really don't know what will happen for true,
They're bound to split me in two!

—"The Mighty Dougla"[1]
Popular Calypso

The dilemma this "dougla"[2] faces in this song parallels what many
people experience when meeting me for the first time. With a last
name like "Chan Tack", they envision a pure Chinese. On being con-
fronted with the flesh, however, they are invariably surprised to see
coffee-brown skin, black-brown curly hair, full lips and a small nose.
It is only the trademark Chinese eyes that give any ring of veracity to
my claim to a Chinese surname.

Being a mixture of many ethnicities: East Indian, Chinese, Spanish,
Portuguese and unidentifiable other, I believe that I am an embodiment
of the "melting pot" that my country, Trinidad, proudly claims to be.
Living in a country as ethnically and hence culturally diverse as Trin-

1 The calypsonian's sobriquet. (A calypsonian is a singer of a certain type of
Trinidadian music called calypso.)
2 Trinidadian colloquialism for children of mixed, especially East Indian and
African, descent

idad and Tobago, and being myself a blend of cultures, has been one of the most significant influences in my life.

Trinidadian[3] society is not racially discriminating, but racially polarized. However, inter-race relations are generally harmonious. Fortunately, I live in a very supportive environment. Despite this, I have often had to field questions like "Anjie, what are you?" This, at first, made me feel uncomfortable. The fact that people were attempting to dissect and qualify who I was disturbed me. I was a "what," not a "who"—an oddity, it seemed. However, I soon realized that these questions were generally not malicious. They were simple expressions of the curiosity of people who were intrigued by my "different"-ness.

Throughout my childhood, "what" I was was never really an issue. As far as I was concerned, my family and friends loved me—the whole person. Today, it is not really an issue, but it has, in fact, affected me most profoundly.

My colorful ethnic heritage has given me a unique perspective of life and of people of different races and religions. My participating in Divali, the Hindu festival of lights, attending Indian weddings and learning to eat rice with chopsticks are all heartwarming and indelible experiences. Such participation in the traditions of the myriad ethnicities of my cultural heritage has left me with little room for any sort of prejudice against others. My experience has thus made me much more open-minded and non-judgemental towards people. It has also whetted my appetite to learn about other cultures and hence has fostered in me an intense desire to travel in order to experience the lifestyles of different peoples. I feel equipped to respect divergent beliefs although I may not understand them. Most of all, I know that the value of a person can only be assessed in his/her entirety.

Some people say that being mixed means that one has no roots, no identity. On the contrary, I have found that my heritage gives me roots

3 A citizen of the Republic of Trinidad and Tobago

branching out in all directions—it does not limit, but rather, enriches the quality of my life and my experiences.

ANALYSIS

Chan Tack's essay is typical of those where the writer discusses identity—what they identify themselves with, their ethnic and racial background, and how their identity has affected their relations with others. In this case, the writer explores her identity in relation to her friends: "I was a 'what' not a 'who'—an oddity, it seemed." Essays of this type can explore experiences with discrimination, a new culture, or how a person's identity has influenced their actions.

This piece effectively conveys to the reader Chan Tack's thoughts on her mixed heritage. We see how she has come to terms with her background by dealing with poignant questions such as "Anjie, what are you?" We can imagine people asking this quite innocently. Fortunately, Chan Tack definitively says that she has grown from her experiences and has risen above the superficial characteristics that caused her friends to ask such questions. She keeps a positive outlook, showing that she has learned and grown from her experiences.

The quotation in the beginning of the essay could have been used more throughout the piece. There might have been more closure to the essay if the quotation had been referred to throughout. Was she "split in two"? How did she overcome these forces? If you include a quotation, be sure to explain and develop it wholly and completely. Don't just stick in an eloquent quotation unless it adds considerably to your piece and is one of the building blocks of your essay. Likewise, to write an effective essay, it is very important for the writer to explain all the statements made throughout the piece. Chan Tack mentions that she "lives in a very supportive environment," but does not illustrate to the reader why this is so. Including a more detailed account of an experience in which her racial background played an important role would have illustrated exactly how Chan Tack came to realize that her heritage "enriches the quality of [her] life."

—Daniel A. Shapiro

"Two Good Friends"

By Paul S. Gutman, who attended a private school in Dallas, Texas.

In the last year and a half, I have lost two good friends. In sixty years, only two departed friends might be a blessing, but I have plenty of time in my future to worry about death and mourning.

On the last day of my 1994 spring break, I came downstairs to hear: "Paul, Dan is dead." I could not comprehend: my friend wasn't sick; in fact, I had seen him two days earlier. We had both stayed at the same hotel in Florida. How could someone nearly my age be dead? He had been killed in a jet-skiing accident. This summer, my parents called me at Georgetown. Without much preamble, my mom told me that Jack, Dan's father, had died. On his way to a dinner, Jack had collapsed from a heart attack.

In the spring of 1994, Dan had been anxious to try jet skiing. I, too, wanted to jet ski, but I found myself too busy qualifying for SCUBA certification to accompany him. Before I left Florida, I waved goodbye to him from a sunny beach. I promised to see him in a few months. Four days later, I visited with a tearful family in cold, wet, dreary New York. The death shocked Dan's friends, and all were in tears. Yet, I could not cry. I didn't know then, and I still don't know why that was.

As I looked into set after set of bloodshot, tear-laden eyes, I felt callous for not accepting the grief and crying. I felt reproached by each and every one of Dan's friends, despite the pain I shared with them. The pain continued to worm into my heart, and it still digs uncomfortably into me when I consider Dan's death. It was especially hard to see Dan's younger brother crying. After all, we are that age where we are supposed to be impervious and believe we are invincible. His sadness has carried over to me; I have never embraced the "I'm going to live forever" attitude, but Dan's death weighs on me because we were so close. On that spring day, I lost a good friend. He was two years my senior: the perfect age difference for a little bit of hero worship. Dan was a vivacious, loving person, and frequently wore a smile as part of his wardrobe. Jack was probably the hardest hit, and he never recovered.

Jack had been a friendly, outgoing man who had driven me to his beach house many times. He always smiled, and was always involved with his sons. At Jack's funeral this summer, I saw his family for the third time in fifteen months. Two of those times, we were in a funeral home and nobody was emotionally stable. Although I know that nobody lives forever, Jack's death troubles me because he was not much older than my father.

The night of Jack's funeral, my mother and my father were plagued by bad dreams, my dad dreaming that he himself had a heart attack. I can only hope that my mother or father does not have to suffer the same torture that Jack and Dan's family is enduring.

I endure a torture of my own: I cannot cry for these two friends— one a peer and the other an adult. Both were role models. They were fine human beings: one whom I wanted to be, and one whom I wanted to become. I want to be as well-rounded a person as Dan. I want to become the successful and happy man, Jack. Their passing hurts more because I cannot cry; the lack of tears seems to be a sort of weakness. I do, however, miss both of them, and I know that, like Jay McInerny writes in *Brightness Falls,* missing someone is a way of spending time with them.

ANALYSIS

This essay is a solid attempt to describe what were obviously two very difficult times in the life of the author. While writing on such a topic is by no means the only way to show an admissions officer the maturity of your life experiences, this is a situation in which the events had a great impact on the applicant, therefore, making them appropriate subject matter for a personal statement.

The essay is especially strengthened by the amount of detail Gutman uses to describe his feelings, when he first learned that his good friend had died and the way these feelings changed as time passed. His description of attending Dan's funeral is especially good because he does not simply tell us he was sad. Gutman challenges the reader to understand and trace his grief, anger and confusion. He repeats this when he describes the death of Dan's father, strengthening the essay even more by both drawing parallels between the two and highlighting how they impacted him differently.

Still, this essay could be improved with tighter writing and better organization, especially in the conclusion. Gutman's reference to his parents toward the end of the essay is somewhat distracting; up until that point, he had been the focal point. The transition into the last paragraph could have been better explained and established, since we do not know what helped the author accept the death of his two friends. Even more importantly, the final reference to an outside author is distracting. Gutman could have made this point on his own without allowing another author to intrude on his very personal essay.

—Georgia N. Alexakis

"The Beast"

By Daniel Myung, who attended a public school in
Lexington, Massachusetts.

For the last seventeen years, I have been struggling to peacefully coexist with the beast residing on my scalp. This beast has been a source of great grief and pain. This beast I am talking about is my curly hair.

Because of this outstanding feature, I was treated like a mutant and a novelty by Flushing, New York's, Korean community. I was a sponge for ridicule, and the envy of every mother who permed her hair or wore mascara. (Yes, even my eyelashes curled.) From the day I picked up my first comb, I made every attempt to kill the hated billows that made my life miserable. I wanted to be like everybody else.

It was not until high school that I rethought my reason to battle the beast. I realized that my hair is a unique attribute, and that my tormentors placed my inferiority complex upon me. Killing the beast would simply show I had succeeded in correcting my "flaw" and was ready to disappear into Korean obscurity. I no longer wanted the dead and lifeless hair that everyone else had. It was time for me to discipline the untamed beast and to define who I am.

Dreadful pictures, like the one on my driver's license, are rare occurrences now, and high humidity no longer scares me. My new approach to the beast has been a great blessing. It has given me the opportunity to appreciate the beauty and versatility of the curl and to discover how living with it has defined my character. By not resigning myself to being an average, limp-locked Korean, I have always sought to put my flair, my "curliness," into all that I do. It is my desire to be the one head that always stands out. As a musician, artist, and student, my greatest fear and obstacle is anonymity.

Any cellist can read music and create pleasant noise, but not all cellists play with emotion. Skill may be present, but flavor—fire—is not. Ever since my beginning days, my playing has always had intensity and passion. This "curl" to my playing is my greatest asset, for even if my skill is lacking, my vigor makes up for it.

This same vigor is also put into my efforts to produce our school's yearbook. Our task is to produce an original, one-of-a-kind book. So many yearbooks I have seen are bland and hardly distinguishable from the next, as if only the pictures were replaced in each one. It is my mission to make our yearbook as original, witty and unique as possible.

ANALYSIS

This essay scores points for taking a more comical approach in describing how the author overcame a major obstacle in his life—his curly hair. While the life experience described is not the most extreme example of hardship and suffering, the applicant uses humor to stand out in the minds of admissions officers and create a memorable essay.

Still, the essay suffers from a common pitfall of many admissions essays: the writer tells his story rather than illustrates it through examples. We rely on the author to tell us he was ridiculed rather than being shown through particularly humiliating scenarios in his life. Such details would have livened up the essay even more, capitalizing on its already humorous subject matter, and given the author a better opportunity to display his skills as a writer and observer.

This lack of detail becomes an even bigger problem when Myung talks about his personal transition from someone who hated his curly hair to someone who came to accept it. This was obviously a life-changing moment for the author, but all we know is that the attitude change came sometime during his high school career.

The need for clear and well-articulated transitions becomes even more important when Myung connects his accepting his physical differences to his excellence in extracurricular activities. The transition between the two subjects is abrupt and the essay ends on an abrupt note as well.

So while the choice of subject matter was original and humorous, this essay could have been made better with more examples from the author's childhood and the formative years in which he came to accept and love his "beast." Because the admissions essays are usually best when short and limited in their scope, Myung might have done better to limit his personal statement to his hair or his cello or the yearbook. Trying to link the three produces an essay with weak transitions and superficial treatment of otherwise interesting subject matter.

—Georgia N. Alexakis

"Between a Rock and Home Plate"

By Mark K. Arimoto, who attended a medium-sized private school in Honolulu, Hawaii.

Athlete." Often the word conjures up the image of a lithe, muscled person with one percent body fat, and able to leap tall buildings in a single bound. I am not this person. In fact, my career as an athlete is not what most consider successful. I have always enjoyed participating in athletics. Whether my ability is equal to my enthusiasm is another story.

My first sport was baseball. I was constantly trying to make up for being the smallest on the team. I would try to swing the bat as hard as my home-run-hitting teammates but my hits would invariably pop skyward or dribble weakly in the vicinity of third base. I would try to throw the ball as far as my cannon-armed fellow outfielders, only to see my coaches run forward so they could pick it up while it was still rolling. About the only thing I could do with any degree of success was run. Small but quick, I would hustle on and off the field, to and from my position, hoping to impress my coaches with my enthusiasm if not with my playing skills.

In the interim between my fifth- and sixth-grade season I worked hard. I knew it would take much more than running around to land a starting position in my final season in the Bronco division. I even attended my school's intermediate baseball tryouts a year early to improve my skills.

On the final day of the intermediate tryouts I reached out to catch a fly ball . . . and felt my thumb crush between the ball and glove. With a broken thumb I would be out for the first half of the season. My hopes for starting felt as crushed as my finger.

However, I continued to persevere and to preserve my faith and the skills I had worked so hard to improve. I read books on fielding and hitting, watched instructional videos, and sat on the sidelines cheering for my team as I waited for my finger to heal.

When at long last I could play again, I was determined to prove to the coaches and to myself that a decent ballplayer lurked in my rather unimpressive 4' 10", eighty-five-pound frame. The weeks of preparation showed in my playing; I still wasn't hitting home runs and my arm still wasn't a cannon, but I would get base hits and the coaches didn't need to run forward to pick up my throws, earning a starting position at centerfield. All too soon it was the final game and we were playing for second place. More than that, we were playing against our rivals, the Yankees. We took the field with all the determination and intensity of the World Series.

The score remained close throughout the game as the ninth inning drew near. In the top of the ninth, we were tied at ten all with two outs and the Yankees' slugger at bat. An image of Mighty Casey, except with a joyous Mudville, ran through my mind as he strode to the plate. Our coaches waved a signal and the outfield played deep. I saw the pitcher slowly wind up while the Yankee behemoth waved his bat behind his head in anticipation. Then the waiting was over. The fastball headed straight for the heart of the strike zone and with a quick, tight swing I heard the crack of the bat. Far from shooting like a rocket as his other hits had, the ball was sailing in a lazy arc heading for the hole I had created by playing deep. I sprinted forward, the noise of the crowd fading in my ears as I focused on the small, falling sphere before me, hoping the drills I had practiced endlessly would help me now. As I drew nearer, I knew my legs wouldn't propel me fast enough to position myself under the ball. Without thinking, I took a final few steps and dove forward.

Rolling as I hit the ground, I jumped to my feet searching the ground for the ball. A second later I opened my glove and found the baseball nestled snugly in the pocket.

We ran off the field jumping up and down, laughing and cheering. It was the bottom of the ninth, our final time at bat for the season, and we were determined to win. Unfortunately, unlike the Yankees, our best hitters were not up to bat. We managed to advance a runner to third base, but not without the cost of two outs. Just as the Yankees had only needed a base hit to score, so did we. But whereas the Yankees had their slugger, the Braves were at the bottom of the order: me.

My hitting had not improved as much as my fielding since last season. Sensing the power in my arms, the infield positioned themselves closer. The pitcher threw the ball. I swung. Strike one! He threw again. Again I swung. Strike two! I stepped out of the batter's box. I thought about all the drills I had practiced, all the books I had read, all the videos I had watched. I thought about all the time I had sat on the sidelines waiting to play. I stepped back into the batter's box and stopped thinking about everything except my hitting drill. Step. Plant. Swing. Follow through. It echoed in my head. I saw the third pitch barrel in. I stepped. I planted. I swung. I followed through. I felt the bat connect. Not looking to see where it flew I ran faster than I ever had before. Standing on first, I turned and saw the ball in the outfield and my teammate on home plate. We had won!

After the game, the team huddled around as the coaches gave their final post-game speech. They congratulated everyone and then turned to me. I had been voted the team's MVP, and they presented me with the "game-winning rock." (The ball I had hit actually belonged to the Yankees.) A few weeks later I received a congratulatory note from my coaches. They talked of my batting average and defensive play, but I was particularly touched when they wrote, "More importantly, your enthusiasm and hustle set the tone for others. You are a natural leader and we thoroughly enjoyed being your coaches."

I realized then that it wasn't my skill so much as my spirit that earned me the rock and the respect of my coaches. I would like to go on to describe how after this incident I went on to become a star player for my school team, but to tell the truth, I was cut twice.

After my baseball endeavors, I was in ninth grade and able to try out for the tennis team. Although I was cut from my new sport two years in a row, I didn't feel badly because I had given it my best. The coach took me aside after cuts and offered me the position of manager. He had seen how I had come to every practice and had played with a lot of heart, if not a lot of skill. I was elated. For me, it was an opportunity to learn the ropes and still practice with the team. In my junior year I tried out for a sport without many cuts, paddling. Just before training went into full swing, I ruptured my tricep volunteering at a service project (making, of all things, kadomatsu, a Japanese New Year symbol of endurance, strength, and good luck). The doctors said it would take four weeks to heal, the season began in three. After talking with the coaches I continued to train with the team. I ran the three miles the team ran for conditioning, then ran another two. I lifted weights in order not to lose strength in my arms as my tricep healed. By the third week I was ready to paddle and rejoined my crew by the second race.

While the paddling team was perennially in last place, it did not detract from my experience with athletics. Indeed, this experience has given me much more than a rock, a note, and a JV letter; it has given me the confidence, strength, and motivation to persevere despite setbacks. It has shown me an inner strength, a spirit that the three "trophies" represent, a spirit born out of love for what I am doing, a spirit that doesn't let doubt and self-pity stand in the way of achieving goals, a spirit that fuels my desire to achieve.

Truly, for me, athletics has been a success, if not in the traditional sense; after all, it's not every day that one receives the game-winning rock.

ANALYSIS

"Between a Rock and Home Plate" is an eloquently written admissions essay in which the applicant describes his trying experiences as an athlete. Immediately pointing out that he does not fit into the mold of the stereotypical "jock," he explains how he never let his size or lack of athletic skill stop him from following his dreams. Through each sporting experience, from Little League baseball to high school tennis, the applicant expresses his enthusiasm and desire to work hard at whatever goal he is trying to accomplish.

The strength of this essay lies in the way it is written. In particular, the precise use of adjectives gives the reader a clear picture of the applicant's struggles to make the team. Also, the use of figurative devices, such as the similes ("My hopes for starting felt as crushed as my finger") and metaphors ("cannon-armed fellow outfielders") help solidify the reader's understanding of the challenges the applicant faced. In turn, the reader gains a firm comprehension of the amount of enthusiasm the applicant has when going after his goals. One common admission essay problem is generality—applicants often try to explain their triumphs in a number of different areas instead of focusing on one topic. While this essay does explain the applicant's determination in a variety of different sports, he does not skimp on details. Each topic gets explained fully and in depth.

The depth and description of each sport the applicant played is commendable; however, the essay is on the long side. The applicant could have chosen to write about either baseball or tennis, but probably should not have chosen both. The climax of the essay comes with the game-winning hit, and shortly thereafter, the essay should probably end. Another improvement might be to remove the two last paragraphs, which describe the lessons learned from sporting experiences. The goal when writing this type of essay is for the stories to express the positive traits of the applicant, without having to list them explicitly. Clearly, these stories express the applicant's positive traits of determination and dedication, so it is unnecessary to summarize them at the end.

—Joshua H. Simon

"Hanging On"

By Susie Yi Huang, who attended a small public high school in
Skillman, New Jersey.

When you get to the end of your rope, tie a knot and hang on.
—*Franklin D. Roosevelt*

I truly learned the meaning of this quotation during the summer I
turned fourteen. Since I aspired to become a doctor, I realized the
importance of completing the most difficult science courses my school
offered. I discussed the option of doubling up on science classes with
several upperclassmen, who discouraged such a route because of the
stress I would already have from taking an intense load of honors and
advanced placement courses. Studying two sciences in one year also
meant that my attention to both would be limited if I had to devote my
time to not one but two of the courses I valued most. Vowing to ease
my course load by taking chemistry over the summer, I enrolled in a
full-credit chemistry course at the Rutgers Preparatory Summer
School. Little did I realize how much I would gain from the experience,
knowledge about not just chemistry but also about myself and life.

From the first day of the course, I recognized how concentrated my
studies would have to be if I wanted to achieve my goal of passing the
class with an A average. My teacher, a Nigerian professor from Rutgers
University with a Ph.D. in chemistry, impressed me as an austere,
rigorous instructor used to dealing with bright college students, not
mere high school students like us. She seemed insensitive to our needs,
although I later realized that she created this façade to push us through
a challenging course. The amount of homework she assigned to us and
the protracted hours we spent in class were disheartening. I had never

followed such a demanding course of study and longed to relax during my summer vacation; instead, I found myself confined in a drab, frigid building day after day. Bitterness grew within me as I completed the first two weeks of the eight-week course.

I found, however, that I could stand the class as long as I did reasonably well in it. I understood the material we covered, and, while my grades were not as high as I would have liked, I believed I could bring my average up to the coveted A. Then the professor began assigning a succession of labs that were to be completed every day following the lecture. Unfamiliar with the laboratory equipment, I stumbled my way through the first few and, as a result, received low C's and D's on the labs, which consequently brought down my entire grades. I became frustrated at my inability to master the lab techniques and at my failure to keep up my grades. The professor's apathy, moreover, troubled me, particularly her cold attitude toward my low lab grades and her unwillingness to address my concerns. Struggling to grasp the lab concepts without the attention that I was accustomed to receiving from my teachers, I questioned whether to continue the course. Since chances seemed slim that I would be able to earn the desired credits, I contemplated dropping out and enjoying the rest of the summer free of work.

Over the following week, I considered my priorities and outlined the possibilities upon which I could act. I could drop out of the course and take it during the school year, but that would mean that I would either have to learn two sciences in one year or simply omit one of the sciences I had planned to take. I could also continue taking the course for no credit, thus easing myself of the pressure I had previously felt. Neither option satisfied me. If I dropped out of the class, I would gain immediate gratification from having the rest of my summer free, but I would need to retake chemistry in school, which countered my original intention. If I took the class for no credit, I would excel in chemistry when I repeated it, but I would still not be able to advance to any other science course without having passed chemistry. The only option left was to complete the course with full credit and earn a grade that reflected my capabilities. I chose to follow this course of action and persevered with a determination I had previously lacked. Despair and occasional frustration did not flee as soon as I chose to see my task out to its completion, but I had a renewed purpose that carried me through my bouts of discouragement: to prove to myself that I had the strength to brave a difficult course and an unyielding instructor.

Despite the extended hours and extra week of summer school I had to attend to earn the desired number of credits, I overcame the difficulties of that chemistry class and passed with an A+ average. Still, I consider the lessons that I gained from my experience to be more meaningful than the good grade I earned. I came into contact with the reality of the adult world as a fourteen-year-old. In confronting a college professor who embodied the academic world beyond the microcosm of high school, I had to adapt to a rigid teaching style by gaining academic independence. I learned not to panic and lose sight of my priorities in the face of conflict but to adhere to my principles of hard work and self-confidence. Instead of balking at failure, I came to understand that I should not fear making mistakes since I gained more from suffering a drop in my grade than from succeeding from the beginning. I now look forward to challenges instead of shying away from them, and I value the determination that guided me through my struggle. My experience helped remove the limits I had set on myself prior to completing the course. By tying a knot when I was at the end of my rope, I was able to pursue my goal with success.

ANALYSIS

This essay takes the reader through a journey of perseverance that demonstrates how the applicant has handled and overcome adverse situations. The type of essay that demonstrates an instance of personal determination and achievement is used quite often but is usually a safe one to do. Most people have had challenges that they have had to overcome. A story on how such a challenge was overcome can usually reveal quite a bit about the writer that will add to one's application.

Throughout her essay, Huang continually demonstrates how she is willing to take on extra work, and make the extra effort to get ahead and overcome her difficulties with the chemistry class. It is made quite clear that Huang is a hard worker and will most likely apply what she has learned from her summer experience to her studies at college. The quotation by FDR adds a nice touch to the essay. It brings together all the experiences and emotions that Huang had gone through during her summer.

Unfortunately, this essay portrays Huang as grade-hungry and obsessed with her classes. Several times Huang mentions her goal of "passing the class with an A average." It is unnecessary and might hurt the application's effectiveness. Why was Huang so focused on doing well in class? Was it because she was truly interested in learning new things, pleasing her parents, or was it a matter of taking pride in her work? A reader would much more prefer learning about one of these things. The extent and difficulty of her courses, as well as her grades, will all be reflected on Huang's transcript. Perhaps including a more specific experience, such as studying for an exam, might make a more favorable impression of the character and personality of the candidate.

—Daniel A. Shapiro

"Joy and Trembling"

By Erin Dana Leib, who attended a middle-sized private high school in
Bronx, New York.

Walking along the tawny shades of desert sands this past summer,
I was engulfed by the vastness that lay ahead. The majestic
environment stood before me, unbound by the fetters of time and seemingly uncluttered by the advent of modernity. Without a single cloud
or cliff to prevent my exposure to the glorious skies overhead, the
claustrophobic emptiness enveloped me. The silence pierced my ears.
The magnitude confounded my eyes and the unprecedented intensity
frightened my soul.

But, alas, amidst the silence, I heard a song. The rhythm of my
pulse began to proclaim my vitality. My blood began to dance, creating
scores of rapid beats. My throbbing heart and trembling feet joined the
desert winds in a symphonic performance. The mellifluous notes forced
me toward contemplation and thrust me toward heaven. They beckoned
me to confront myself, to hear my own voice calling to me through the
daunting desert silence. They asked me to feel for a moment the power
of the moment, to locate the Divine in the sublimity of the environment
that surrounded me. As William Wordsworth said in his poem "Lines
Composed a Few Miles Above Tintern Abbey," "While with an eye
made quiet by his power/Of harmony, and the deep power of joy,/ We
see into the life of things." And I did.

Like the beloved river of Hesse's *Siddhartha,* the desert allowed me
to hear "voices of pleasure and sorrow, good and evil, laughing and
lament . . ." only after years of relatively deaf existence. Indeed, I journeyed along several inadequate paths to find the synthesis of joy and
trembling, passion and reason, that I encountered in the desert.

For years I have struggled with the age-old conflict between the life
of the body and the life of the mind. As a child who was invested in

truly celebrating life, I indulged in an existence replete with passion. Paralleling Siddhartha's life as a rich man, I submerged myself in worldly experiences in an attempt to live every moment of my life actively. I operated spontaneously, caring not for the past or future, but only for the present. Indeed, I spent much of my time dancing, never taking time even to plant my feet on the ground. There was a genuine joy that overwhelmed my soul then and a radiance that consequently surrounded me.

But,

That time is past,
And all its aching joys are now no more,
And all its dizzy raptures. Not for this
Faint I, nor mourn no murmur; other gifts
Have followed, for such a loss, I would believe
Abundant recompence
    —Wordsworth, "Lines Composed a Few Miles Above Tintern Abbey"

With time, that life of the body could no longer satisfy my cravings. That mode of existence had deafened me to the intellectual callings of my mind. The triviality of living only for transient earthly pleasure became painfully clear, as I continually re-encountered my own void. And so I happily immersed myself in the rational life of the mind. While Siddhartha opted to join the Samanas, a group of ascetic monks, "to let the Self die . . . to experience pure thought," I chose to reorient my connections to the world in order to let my self live. No longer did my involvement with the world extend only to that which was apparent or knowable. Rather, I thirsted for all that lay beyond my limited view. Questions of religion and philosophy began to consume my mind, as the world of theory and of abstraction became my home. I approached all of my pursuits with rigid rationality, constantly evaluating the validity of all that I encountered. Complexities and inconsistencies continuously plagued me, and I reveled in the rigor of the intellectual life.

Despite the excitement of this purely rational existence, it too had deafened me, for in my attention to inconsistency, the wholeness of the melody of the encounter had often been obscured. I yearned to hear the music now. I desired the synthesis of my words of passion and reason in order to emerge a more consummate being. Indeed, as Socrates said, "The unexamined life is not worth living." But, with increasing certainly, I also knew that the unlived life was not worth examining. It was with this awareness that I entered the desert.

I approached the arid land fearing that my separation from the days of my youth would prevent me from imbibing its power. My childhood had allowed me to savor the beauty of nature, and I suspected that my rationality would no longer allow for such recognition. Yet Siddhartha's journey again mirrored my own, for it was in the natural world that I found a potent fusion of mind and body. The intellect and the soul became indistinguishable there, as my initial trembling gave way to ecstatic joy, provoking further trembling. The animated songs of my pulse merged with the daunting calls for confrontation with both the self and the Divine. Like Siddhartha's experience, " . . . the lament of those who yearn, the laughter of the wise, the cry of indignation, and the groan of the dying. They were all interwoven and interlocked entwined in a thousands ways." As I left the desert, I celebrated the pleasure and the pain of my enhanced listening,

For I have learned
To look on nature, not as in the hour
Of thoughtless youth, but hearing oftentimes
That still, sad music of humanity,
Not harsh, not grating, though of ample power
To chasten and subdue. And I have felt
A presence that disturbs me with the joy
Of elevated thoughts; a sense sublime
Whose dwelling is the light of setting suns,
And the round ocean, and the living air,

And the blue sky . . .
> —Wordsworth, *"Lines Composed a Few Miles Above Tintern Abbey"*

ANALYSIS

This essay has an intellectual and thoughtful tone, which effectively articulates the writer's understanding of herself relative to her world. The continuous references to Wordsworth's poem, as well as Hesse and Socrates, demonstrates a strong literary ability to gather evidence to support her topic ideas. In addition, the direct quoting of selections from Woodsworth's poem reveals the writer's ability to summarize details and comprehend overall themes. Immediately, the reader recognizes that this writer has strong skills to synthesize multiple sources for critical thinking and analysis, which are certainly important abilities for success in college.

The essay is well structured with organized development of the writer's initial realization of freedom in the introductory paragraph, the progression of hearing an inner song, the expounding of her existence, to her celebratory conclusion in which the reader is swept in the writer's growth and vitality. Indeed, the images of this essay are clear as the author is careful to paint continuous visions of herself, the natural sphere, and the key integration of those two worlds. Along the way, we feel the energy of the writer as she makes multiple references to her interest in dance as a metaphor to the vitality of life.

Ultimately, the most important achievement of this essay is that the writer shares with you her thinking process in the middle paragraphs, allowing the reader to know her best by illustrating how she evaluates a given situation. The writer shares her excitement and enthusiasm as well as her strong command of literary analysis, all encompassed in a revelation of her inner energy.

> —Nancy Poon

POINTS OF
VIEW

"On Diplomacy in Bright Nike Running Tights"

By Christopher M. Kirchhoff, who attended a public high school in suburban Columbus, Ohio.

B eepbeep.
Beepbeep.

Beepbeep. With a series of subtle but relentless beeps, my faithful Timex Ironman watch alarm signaled the start of another day, gently ending the pleasant slumber I so often fail to enjoy. With the touch of a button I silenced the alarm, falling back on my bed to establish a firmer grasp of where I was and why on earth I had set my alarm for 5:45 A.M. Slowly the outline of my soundly sleeping roommate came into focus. Beyond his bed was the window. Across the Neva River the view of the Hermitage and Winter Palace, illuminated brightly with spotlights, faded in and out of the falling snow. I was definitely still in St. Petersburg, and no, this wasn't a dream. "Oh yes, running," I remembered. "Must go running."

Temperature??? I dialed the front desk. "Kakoy tempatura pozholsta." Not fooled by my Berlitz Russian, the voice responded, "Negative 7 degrees" in crisp English. I reached for my running tights, glad that meant negative seven degrees Celsius. I took another look into the darkness outside. Negative seven degrees Fahrenheit and I would not be running. The hotel lobby was empty except for the guard and the woman at the desk. As I stepped outside, I pressed the start button on my Timex Ironman and began jogging.

It was a pristine morning. The November wind promptly reminded me just what winter meant at 60 degrees north latitude. With the sky awaiting the break of dawn, I started making my way through the newly fallen snow. Soon the sound of my labored breathing came through the rhythmic swooshing of running shoes dancing through the snow. As clouds of breath collected in front of me, I passed slowly through them, marking my forward progress with each exhale. Around the corner I found a freshly shoveled sidewalk. Following the inviting path, I soon came upon the shoveler, an old man sporting the classic Russian winter outfit: fur cap, long coat, and mittens. Time had left its mark on his wrinkled face and worn clothing. Despite the falling snow, which accumulated at a far greater pace than the man could keep up with, he continued to shovel relentlessly, barely glancing up as I jogged by him. I respect his perseverance. He was working fiercely in the Russian spirit. And as the war medals proudly displayed on his coat indicate, he had been doing so for a while. Perhaps this man was one of the few that survived the Nazi siege on Leningrad, a living reminder of why the United States must remain deeply involved in world politics.

As I turned and ran across the bridge leading downtown, the battleship *Potemkin* came into view. The *Potemkin* began the second Russian Revolution by training its guns on the Winter Palace. Still afloat as a working museum, young sailors in full military dress cleared its decks of snow. While I ran past the ship, a sailor stopped to wave. As his inquisitive eyes stared into mine, we both recognized each other's young age. I waved back, shouting, "Doebroyah ootra," wishing him a good morning. A few seconds later I glanced back, noticing that the same sailor was still looking at me. I must have been quite a sight in my brightly colored Nike running suit treading through a foot of new snow. "How ironic," I thought, "here stands a high school aged Russian sailor shoveling snow off a ship which I studied in history class, while each of us is equally bewildered at the other's presence."

By the time I reached the Hermitage the sky was clear enough to see my reflection in the cold black of the Neva River. While running past the Winter Palace, I quickened my pace, half expecting the Tsarina to step out and stop my progress. I sprinted through Revolution Square, glancing left to see the spot where Tsar Nicolas abdicated and right to see the monument commemorating the defeat of Napoleon. While trodding through historic St. Petersburg, I reflected on the last discussion I had with Sasha, my Russian host student. Sasha, top in his class in the "diplomatic" track of study, had talked about his political beliefs for the first time. What begun as a question-and-answer session about life in the United States became a titanic struggle between political ideals. Sasha's tone and seriousness clearly indicated that our discourse was not for pleasure. He wanted to know about our government and what democracy meant for him and his people. Being the first U.S. citizen Sasha had ever met, I felt obligated to represent my country as best I could. Realizing that my response could forever shape his impression of democracy in the U.S., the importance of my mission as a student ambassador became even more apparent.

For Russians, democracy remains a new and untrusted method of government. Clearly, Russia is still in a state of change, vulnerable to the forces of the past and skeptical of the future. Sasha, unable to share my faith in the democratic political process, listened patiently to my explanations. I tried my best to help Sasha conceptualize what the United States is about and just what it means to be an American. For the sake of both countries I hope he accepted my pro-democracy arguments. It was conversations like these that brought a new sense of urgency to my time in Russia. Through the course of my visit, Sasha and I came to know each other and each other's people. His dream of serving as a diplomat may very well materialize. Perhaps someday Sasha will be in a position to make decisions that affect the United States. I hope my impression will in some way affect his judgment in a positive manner.

After jogging up the hotel steps, I pressed the stop button. Not bad for a morning run I thought. Sixty-four minutes in deep snow, about seven miles' worth. Press Mode button. Time zone one: E.S.T. Columbus, Ohio. It was Saturday night back home. Thinking of home, I remembered the student in my homeroom who cried, "You mean you're gonna go and meet those Commies? So you think you can change the world?" Press Mode button.

Time zone two: St. Petersburg, Russia, November 4, 1995. Greeting the dawn of a new day I thought, "Perhaps! Perhaps in some small way I can change the world, one conversation at a time."

ANALYSIS

The month that Christopher Kirchhoff spent in Russia as a "student diplomat" undoubtedly provided him with more than enough experiences to include in an admissions application. But in his essay "On Diplomacy in Bright Nike Running Tights," Kirchhoff successfully avoids falling into the trap of many applicants whose statements are based on once-in-a-lifetime opportunities.

Kirchhoff easily could have written something along the lines of, "My time in Russia provided me with a rare opportunity to witness an emerging democracy grappling with its newfound freedom. Armed with a keen interest in the post-Communist plight, I set forth to learn from my Russian brethren and to teach them about their American peers." These statements are not necessarily untrue, but they are also not especially original. Such an essay would hardly stand out among a stack of statements written by students retelling the glory of winning the state debate/football/academic challenge championship.

Instead, Kirchhoff tells the admissions committee about the Russia he has come to know on his early-morning jogs. We learn that he is a disciplined runner, a perceptive observer of human nature, a willing learner of the Russian language. Bright Nike running tights, his Timex Ironman, and the rhythmic swooshing of his running shoes are details that his audience will remember. They also provide the perfect segue into the more substantive issues Kirchhoff wants to address in his essay—the conversations he has had with Russians his age. The reader gets to know Kirchhoff before we get to know his views on such weightier subjects as diplomacy and the American role in international relations.

While his supposedly verbatim thoughts after waving to the young sailor sound stilted ("How ironic . . . each of us is equally bewildered at the other's presence"), Kirchhoff's understated and personal approach throughout the majority of his essay makes up for his waxing a bit too eloquent at times. Ideally, it would have been nice to hear just as much detail about his conversations with Sasha as we do about St. Petersburg at 6 A.M. The essay loses the details when it matters most. Also in terms of detail, Kirchhoff makes a slight error in his statement that "the *Potemkin* began the second Russian Revolution by training its guns on the Winter Palace." It was in fact the *Aurora* that fired mostly blank rounds on the palace—the battleship *Potemkin* was the scene of a 1905 revolt by sailors in Odessa. These mistakes are rather minor since the essay is not particularly centered on the ship. However, let this serve as a valuable lesson: it is important to extensively check all facts used in your essay.

Still, Kirchhoff's essay works.

—Georgia N. Alexakis

"The Tug of War"

By Kiratiana E. Freelon, who attended a large public school in
Chicago, Illinois.

I stand between two men. The caramel-skinned man on my left holds
his cane as if the world is waiting for his entrance. On my right the
taller vanilla-skinned man stands erect as if he must carry the world.
Each man reaches for my hand and before long, a tug-of-war ensues
between them. Each tries to pull me over the line of agreement but my
body stays in the middle. During this struggle I hear their voices saying:

"Cast down your bucket where you are!"

"The problem of the twentieth century is the problem of the color
line!"

"It is at the bottom we must begin, not at the top!"

"The only way we can fully be men is with the acquisition of social
equality and higher education!"

Their voices blur. My torso stretches wider and wider. My arms grow
in length as each man pulls and pulls. Finally, I yell, "I can't take it
anymore!"

This is the scene that plays in my head when I contemplate the philosophies of Booker T. Washington and W. E. B. Du Bois, two foes attempting to answer a question that never seems to go away: "How shall
the African-American race be uplifted?" Their answers represented
the right and left of the social spectrum in the early 1900s. I attempted
to present their views in the IB Extended Essay. While I wrote the paper something inside of me felt the need to agree with and choose one
philosophy over the other. I couldn't. So this struggle developed.

In the beginning, Washington looked as if he had already lost the
tug-of-war. When I first encountered the ideas of Washington I wanted
to grab him and ask him, "What was going through your head?" The
former-slave-turned-leader-of-a-race, Washington advocated indus-

trial education over higher education. When he said, "cast down your bucket," he meant relinquishing social equality in the name of economic prosperity. When I read this, one word popped into my mind, "Uncle Tom." I felt that Washington had betrayed his race when he renounced social equality. Wasn't that a right every man wanted?

After examining Washington, examining Du Bois was like jumping into a hot bath after sliding headfirst through a field of cow dung. The intellectual's ideas of higher education and social equality sat well with my middle-class African-American stomach. Du Bois represents everything I grew up admiring. Du Bois was the radical who attended Harvard University. His idea of a "talented tenth" to lead the African-American race starkly resembles the black middle class today. I had no choice but to agree with Du Bois.

So enamored with Du Bois was I that I forgot about Washington's practical ideas of self-help and economic power. I witnessed Washington's ideas acted out in everyday life. I bought my "black" hair products from an Asian owner in the middle of the ghetto and the corner store owned by Iranians supplied me with chips and candy. These facts made me feel that maybe African-Americans had shoved Washington too far back into the closet. At this juncture, Washington began to give Du Bois competition in a formerly one-sided war. Economic prosperity means power; a race with economic power cannot be denied social equality, right?

In order to resolve the dilemma presented by this tug-of-war, I looked at the ingredients of my life. Washington appealed to the part of me that wanted to forget about social equality. That part of me wanted to live as it came and focus only on self-advancement. Du Bois appealed to the part of me that felt no man was a man without social equality. Either way, both appealed to my life as an African-American. The fact that two early twentieth-century advocates affected a '90s African-American girl shows that their message was not lost in the passage of time.

Neither man won the tug-of-war. Maybe this tug-of-war in my head was not meant to be won because their philosophies influenced me equally. Washington provided the practical ingredients for social advancement while Du Bois provided the intellectual ingredients for such advancement. African-Americans must evaluate both philosophies and determine how both views can facilitate the advancement of the race. I still stand between two men but now I embrace them equally.

ANALYSIS

The question of racial identity can be an enormous one for many people and often makes a great college essay. Writing an essay about this part of your development is insightful into your person and your views. Admissions officers are trying to get to a portrait of who you are and what you value, and little is more revealing than a struggle for racial identity. Freelon chose to write about two black leaders to show what her racial identity means to her. Her essay also shows a keen interest in how history can be applied to her life—an interest that would appeal to admissions officers trying to pick thoughtful individuals.

Freelon's essay is well written and well organized. She moves smoothly from her opening thoughts into the body of the essay and devotes equal time to each philosophy. She also shows clear examples of why she originally liked Du Bois and why she changed her mind about Washington. Her essay shows important elements of human nature—she admits that as a "middle-class African-American," she has a bias, and she is also wrong from time to time.

The main danger in this essay is oversimplification. It's difficult to condense the arguments of two leaders into a few paragraphs, and Freelon doesn't present the total view of their philosophies. She also assumes a familiarity on the part of the admissions officer with issues of racial identity, which may or may not be true. Overall, however, Freelon's essay is an excellent example of how a personal identity struggle can reveal a lot about the person inside.

—Caille M. Millner

"Salade Olivier"

By Svetlana Rukhelman, who attended a large public high school in
Newton, Massachusetts.

F or as long as I can remember, there was always the *salade Olivier*.
It consisted of boiled potatoes, carrots, eggs, bologna and pickles
diced into tiny cubes and mixed into a giant enamel pot together with
canned peas and mayonnaise. It was considered a delicacy, and prepared only on special occasions such as birthday and dinner parties.
But it was also a ritual, the only component of the first course which
was never absent from a dinner table, no matter which of our relatives
or friends was throwing the feast.

Ironically, the *salade Olivier* was never my favorite food, though the
attitude of my taste buds to the dish did evolve through the years. In
my earliest childhood, I favored the compliant potatoes, then began to
lean toward the pickles and bologna—that sweet-and-sour, crunchy-
and-soft combination that never loses its appeal—and next passed a
phase in which the green peas appeared so abhorrent that I would
spend twenty minutes picking every pea I could find out of my serving.
Only recently did I resign myself to the fact that all the ingredients
must be consumed simultaneously for maximum enjoyment as well as
for the sake of expediency.

It may seem odd, then, to be writing in such length in praise of a
dish one does not particularly like. But culinary memories are determined not so much by whether we found a food tasty, but by the events,
people, and atmospheres of which the food serves as a reminder. In
my mind, the very making of the *salade* has always been associated
with the joyful bustle that accompanied the celebrations for which the
dish was prepared: the unfolding of the dinner table to its full length,
the borrowing of chairs from neighbors, the starched white tablecloths,
simmering crystal wineglasses, polished silverware, white napkins,

delicate porcelain plates of three different sizes stacked one on top of another, the aroma floating from the kitchen all through the apartment, my father taking me on special shopping errands, the wonderful dilemma of "what to wear?" and myriad other pleasant deviations from the monotony of everyday existence. Though simple in theory, the preparation of the *salade Olivier* was a formidable undertaking which occupied half the morning and all but one of the stove burners. At first it was my responsibility to peel the boiled potatoes—the one task which did not require the use of a knife or other utensil, and one which I performed lovingly, albeit inefficiently. As I sat at the kitchen table, my five-year-old fingers covered in several layers of potato skin, my mother and I would lead heart-to-heart discussions, whose topics I no longer remember, but of which I never tired.

Eventually, my mother introduced me to the Dicing of the Potatoes, and then to the Dicing of the Bologna, the Dicing of the Pickles, the Shelling of the Eggs and the Stirring in of the Mayonnaise as well. But there was one stage of the process I found especially mesmerizing. It was the Dicing of the Eggs, carried out one hard-boiled egg at a time with the help of an egg-cutter. Nothing was more pleasing to the eye than the sight of those seven wire-like blades, arranged like prison bars, slicing through the smooth, soft ellipsoid.

Today, we still make the *salade Olivier* on some formal occasions, and, as before, I sometimes participate. And every time I see the egg-slicer or smell the pickles, I am reminded of our Kiev apartment, of those much-anticipated birthday parties, of the joy I felt as I helped my mother cook: of all the things which made my childhood a happy one.

ANALYSIS

This essay seeks to introduce us to the author via a description of the author's childhood conditions and family experiences as well as experiences from the author's cultural heritage. The *salade Olivier,* a delicacy in both Ukrainian and Russian diets, serves as the central organizational motif for this description.

The essay's power comes from its amazing descriptive qualities. The reader is given a vivid and detailed picture of both the *salade* and much of the author's childhood. The essay also entices the reader by deliberately omitting a description of the *salade*'s cultural origins until the very end of the text. This technique forces the reader to move through the essay with puzzling questions about the *salade*'s origins and the reader's unfamiliarity with such a dish, motivating the reader to remain engrossed in the work and seek out the answers of interest. Only in the end are things revealed, and even then the reader may not be fully satisfied.

Despite the essay's great descriptive powers, however, the reader is given few specific details about the author or the Ukrainian culture that serves as the backdrop for the author's childhood. Including more such details could dramatically increase the essay's strength, especially given the unfamiliarity of most readers with the culture that stands at the core of the author's heritage.

—Elliot Shmukler

"Introducing Clark Kent and Willy Wonka"

By Daniel G. Habib, who attended a small Catholic high school in
New York City.

My childhood passions oscillated between two poles: St. Cathe-
rine's Park and the 67th Street branch of the New York Public
Library. Located across Sixty-seventh Street from one another, the two
crystallized the occupations of my youth. On a typical day, I moved
between a close-knit group of friends at the park to largely solitary
stays at the library. My recreational pursuits were communal; my intellectual pursuits were individual. The gulf was pronounced: friends
rarely joined my mother and me as we meandered among the stacks,
and the books I obtained from the library never accompanied me to
the basketball courts or the jungle gym. Generally, I slipped away from
the park during a lull in the action and returned as stealthily as I had
gone, foisting Roald Dahl paperbacks on my mother and scrambling
to rejoin my friends in arguing the relative merits of the Hulk and
Superman. I never thought to integrate these passions; they remained
firmly segregated. That Clark Kent and Willy Wonka should never
cross paths was a given; the giants existed in separate realms of my
life.

More than anything else, my Regis career has reversed that as-
sumption. I now recognize that my intellectual growth and my peer
community are inextricably linked. I have come to regard those who
surround me not simply as a network of friends, but most vitally as
components in the ongoing work of education. I understand that an
individualized process of learning is intellectually impoverished.

The most startling of my educational epiphanies have occurred in the
context of fellow students. Case in point: my acquaintance with Albert
Camus' absurdist manifesto, *The Stranger*. My first reading of the classic,

in sixth grade, came in an atomized intellectual climate. As a result, my understanding of Camus' philosophy was tenuous, so much so that, feeling incapable of defending or even articulating my interpretation of the work, I eschewed any discussion and shunned the chance for error. Satisfied in my ignorance, I disdainfully explained to my inquiring parents, "Oh, it wasn't much of a murder mystery. You know who kills the Arab all along. And that whole mother angle just doesn't fit." My second encounter with Camus came in my junior French IV elective, this time in the company of an insightful octet of Francophones. As we grappled with Camus' vision of the absurd world and Meursault's statement of revolt, an understanding emerged from the sun-drenched Algerian beach. Each member of the class offered his insights for consideration, risking the scrutiny of the group but confident in its intellectual generosity. The rigorous standards of the class, and our common desire for understanding, led eventually to firmer comprehension. My balanced interpretation of Camus derived only from the intensity of discussion, the contributions of my peers, and our mutual willingness to share our insights.

Through my participation in Regis' Speech and Debate Society, I have continued in my quest for the acquisition of knowledge through the group. Extemporaneous Speaking requires that a speaker provide a thorough analysis of a current events/policy proposition, after considering and synthesizing numerous sources. Speakers engage each other on subjects ranging from democratic and free-market reforms in Boris Yeltsin's Russia to the prospects for a Medicare overhaul in the Republican Congress. Practices involve evaluation by fellow team members and success depends intimately on an accurate common understanding of the issues. Lincoln-Douglas Debate, similarly, entails team formulations of argument based on philosophical principles. We prepare as a team, and I have been privileged to benefit from teammates' sophisticated applications and elucidations of issues as diverse as social contract theory and international ethical mandates.

The group character of the team's intellectual strivings was brought to bear most strongly at the Harvard Invitational, in the winter of my junior year. Debaters were asked to evaluate the proposition that "American society is well-served by the maintenance of a separate culture for the deaf." The evening before the tournament began, sixteen debaters massed in one hotel room at the Howard Johnson's on Memorial Drive, and, fueled by peanut butter and marshmallow sandwiches and gallons of coffee, we wrangled over the specifics of the unique resolution. The assimilationist camp suggested that the achievement of group dignity and a private identity for the deaf had to occur against the backdrop of a larger public identity. The separatism inherent in ASL or deaf schools fatally divorced the group from meaningful participation in the American democracy. True cultural uniqueness required a common frame of reference. Conversely, the deaf separatist partisans maintained that this decidedly marginalized minority deserved a distinctness of culture commensurate with the distinctness of its experience. Separation allowed dignity and empowerment.

As the hours wore on and the dialectic raged out of control, positions became more entrenched, but paradoxically a truer comprehension arose. The eloquence and persuasiveness with which each side advanced its interpretation furthered the exchange. We acknowledged and respected the logic of those with whom we disagreed, and we reinforced our own convictions by articulating and defending them. At 1:30, bedraggled, exhausted, and happily not unanimous in perspective, we regretfully dispersed to our rooms, to sleep off the effects of the session.

If I began my educational career as an intellectual monopolist, I have evolved into a collectivist. On our last day of summer vacation, a dozen Regis students spent an afternoon in the Yankee Stadium bleachers, arguing the possible outcomes of the American League pennant race, then returned to Manhattan's Central Park to attend the New York Shakespeare Festival's arresting and hyper-controversial production of *Troilus and Cressida.* As we exited the Delacorte Theater, we reflected on the modernization of Shakespeare's message. Some praised its transmission of bleakness and pessimism; others joined critics in attacking its excesses and its artistic license in manipulating the original. Our consensus on the Bronx Bombers' chances in October was firmer than that on the Greek conquest of Troy, but the essential truth remains. Regis has wonderfully fused the communal and the intellectual phases of my life.

ANALYSIS

Writing about an outstanding learning experience is a fairly common approach to the personal statement. But while many applicants may choose a defining and distinct moment—winning the state speech tournament or setting the school record for the highest GPA—as an experience worth retelling, Habib instead chooses to chronicle the gradual process of intellectual maturation. By choosing this topic, Habib has the opportunity to reflect on his education and recount several formative experiences, not just resort to trite descriptions of winning or losing.

Habib's thesis—that one's communal life and intellectual pursuits are only enhanced when fused together—is a somewhat abstract and difficult argument to make, at least for a high school senior. The fact that Habib makes the argument successfully, through the use of details and concrete examples, makes the essay all the more impressive.

Still, the essay isn't perfect. It's long. The sentences can be complex and a bit convoluted. The language used, while enough to impress any Kaplan SAT instructor, could be toned down to make the essay more reader-friendly. Habib could have easily shortened his statement by using fewer examples of real-life learning experiences. Or the experiences he shares could have been shortened: the admissions committee may not need to know the exact arguments and counter-arguments Habib's Lincoln-Douglas debate team drafted for the Harvard tournament.

Overall, Habib's essay helps distinguish him from other applicants by taking an interesting approach to a common theme and using concrete supporting arguments. All in all, it is a well-written essay enhanced by personal insights, examples, and the all-important details.

—Georgia N. Alexakis

"Sound of Music"

By Alexander Young, who attended a small public high school in
Miami, Florida.

As I fill out this application, I hear music no one else can hear.
Immediately, I sit back, close my eyes, and savor every sound in
an effort to make sense of the notes. Slowly, the music grows louder
and louder—fragments piece together in perfect harmony. The inces-
sant flow of tones saturates my mind, my body, and my soul; this song
is more beautiful than any I have ever heard. My immediate surroundings fade as the music carries me to another level; and briefly, I experience the world of impulsive artistic creation in which Mozart and
Picasso lived.

During these moments, I focus on all the emotions I feel, whether
they are positive or negative. Then, I amplify these feelings and relive
the experience which evoked them, realizing that every moment,
whether of contentment or frustration, is valuable as a life experience
that serves as an inspiration for my music. Depending on the situation,
I may hear the resonance of a violin duet, the timbre of a flute, or the
sonority of a concert piano.

The sounds of music commence during times of personal reflection,
when I am in my room reading a letter, on the Metro-rail observing the
transient masses, or at Matheson Hammock watching the boats float
back to shore. Often, I conscientiously make an effort to further understand and experience other perspectives through thought and imagination. After interacting with people whose lives are remarkably
dissimilar from my own—whether it is a homeless man at Camillus
House or a former Taiwanese political prisoner who helped to transform
a nation—I feel an urge to "look through their eyes" and "feel what
they have felt." Through every interaction and experience, I am in-
creasingly amazed by the disparate world in which we live; this realization also provides the stimulus for the creation of my music.

When the music comes to me, I write down the notes as fast as I can. The beauty of this process is knowing that the world has never heard this creation before. Also, I realize that unless the notes are recorded, the music will never be heard again, because the situation and emotions that give it life are unique to me and this point in time. As I write down the music that only I can hear, I leave a piece of myself to the world—an everlasting record of my being at this moment in time.

ANALYSIS

Young submitted this essay with one of his own compositions—a novel touch. He takes care to communicate his passion for writing music, and his committment to spontaneity, in language that reinforces his goals. Present tense narratives such as his are immediately involving and invite careful reading.

Young effectively touches on other life experiences in the course of his essay, and alludes to knowledge about other artists. He allows the reader to appreciate his sensitive receptivity to creative impulse, and to other people.

Young's conclusion is weaker than the other parts of his essay. There is typically no reason for a college applicant to make a claim to artistic permanence. The final paragraph would improve with the omission of references to "the world." Fundamentally, though, Young succeeds at the basic task of every college essay: making one's self seem lively and interesting.

—Matthew A. Carter

"History as Calculus"

By Jesse Field, who attended a selective state-run math and science college-level program in San Antonio, Texas.

As far back as I can remember, I have wanted to be a scientist. Lately I have done a lot of thinking about what divides sciences like physics and mathematics, slowly realizing that the divisions are merely a convenience we use to name our specialities; all the information discovered in any field is a piece of our ever-growing, ever-resolving model of the universe. It is this model that unites people; all races in all cultures can improve the model. We do so by observing its parts, then adding more, taking some off or improving the ones there, as we see fit. Certainly, then, the question "When will the model be finished?" comes to mind. When time can be described in any situation, when solution methods for partial differential equations are completely generalized in one theory, when a quantum theory of gravity is stumbled upon, when frictional forces like those that make a match flare are described on the atomic and subatomic level, in other words, not in the near future. I personally find this very reassuring; history demonstrates that we need never fear running out of problems to solve.

Leo Tolstoy once described history as analogous to calculus. To him, humanity ebbed and flowed in a series of events and actions that reminded him of a continuous function. Finding the motivations and causes was then, to him, like integrating a continuous function: the sum of "the differential of history, that is, the individual tendencies of men." I find in this a fascinating example for the behavior of us all: to solve the problems of tomorrow, we will have to connect areas of knowledge previously isolated from each other. It has already been happening for years; in the future the process will most likely accelerate. For example, imagine biology today without any input at all from higher mathematics, computer modeling, or theoretical chemistry. The progress made in biology in recent years requires knowledge developed in these fields and others. As it stands now, mathematicians can look forward both to answering questions in their own fields as well as providing input for problems in all other fields of knowledge. This, more than anything else, is what I want to do.

It now seems a simple and reasonable conclusion that the best career choice for me is in mathematics; this was not always so. It was in sixth grade, at age eleven, that I made the sudden and stunning realization that mathematics was not merely a long set of rules regarding addition, subtraction, multiplication, and division. My math teacher had started presenting peculiar math problems of the sort I had noticed before in my own everyday pursuits: problems that required one to work backwards inverting operations to discover an unknown. I was excited at the time because I could see that generalizing this type of problem into different, exact methods for finding the solutions was an extremely important task. From the school library I checked out a book called *The Realm of Algebra* by Isaac Asimov to find out more about this. The true enormity of mathematics struck me when Asimov described the evolution of the complex number system.

What did mathematicians do when they found that no real numbers can be squared to give a negative real numbers? Not acknowledging any former precepts, they simply invented more numbers. It seemed to me that they had to break rules to do this; I found out later that much scientific progress is made by breaking old rules and tossing out old ideas. Since I have always very much enjoyed questioning old ideas and breaking rules, I knew then that I would have to pursue this subject further. Mathematics now seems to me to be a peculiar mix of things invented and things discovered. Studying it and making progress in it requires both inspiration on a par with that required to write good poetry, and the strict adherence to logic which is necessary to persuade one's peers. All in all, I do not doubt the subject's capacity to intrigue me (and thousands of others) for centuries.

ANALYSIS

Field's essay is an articulate exploration of the development of an academic interest in mathematics. The essay is particularly striking because the entire package shows that Field is well-rounded: a technical topic written in an engaging and literary style. The ideas presented in the essay are thought-provoking ways to think about mathematics. By analogizing mathematics to history and poetry, Field demonstrates a certain sophistication in that understanding mathematics in the larger sphere of human knowledge, rather than as a narrowly defined field. The essay also has a pleasant balance of the abstract and concrete personal experiences. While the prose in the middle of the essay is thought out and carefully crafted, both the introduction and ending have a bit of a "tacked on" feel. In addition, the transition to the last paragraph of how choosing his career is "a simple and reasonable conclusion" is also slightly awkward. The essay reads as though paragraphs were written independently and then sewn together at the end. Spend time on your introduction and conclusion as they are the first and last impression the reader receives.

—Jennifer 8. Lee

"Thoughts Behind a Steam-Coated Door"

By Neha Mahajan, who attended a public high school in
Boulder, Colorado.

Till taught by pain Men really know not what good water's worth.
—*Lord Byron*

A light gauze of steam coats the transparent door of my shower. The
temperature knob is turned as far as it can go, and hot drops of
water penetrate my skin like tiny bullets. The rhythm of water dancing
on the floor creates a blanket of soothing sound that envelops me,
muffling the chaotic noises of our thin-walled house. Tension in my
back that I didn't even know existed oozes out of my pores into streams
of water cascading in glistening paths down my body. I breathe in a
mist of herbal scented shampoo and liquid Dove soap, a welcome
change from the semi-arid air of Colorado. In the shower I am alone.
No younger siblings barging unannounced into my room, no friends
interrupting me with the shrill ring of the telephone, no parents nagging
me about finishing college essays.

The ceramic tiles that line my bathroom wall have the perfect coefficient of absorption for repeated reflections of sound waves to create
the wonderful reverberation that makes my shower an acoustic dream.
The two by four stall is transformed into Carnegie Hall as Neha Mahajan, world-renowned musician, sings her heart out into a shampoo
bottle microphone. I lose myself in the haunting melisma of an aalaap,
the free singing of improvised melodies in classical Indian music. I
perfect arrangements for a capella singing, practice choreography for
Excalibur, and improvise songs that I will later strum on my guitar.

Sometimes I sit in the shower and cry, my salty tears mingling with the clear drops upon my face until I can no longer tell them apart. I have cried with the despair of my friend and mentor in the Rape Crisis Team when she lost her sister in a vicious case of domestic abuse, cried with the realization of the urgency of my work. I have cried with the inevitable tears after watching *Dead Poet's Society* for the seventh time. I have cried with the sheer frustration of my inability to convince a friend that my religious beliefs and viewpoints are as valid as hers. Within these glass walls I can cry, and my tears are washed away by the stinging hot water of the shower.

The water that falls from my gleaming brass showerhead is no ordinary tap water. It is infused with a mysterious power able to activate my neurons. My English teachers would be amazed if they ever discovered how many of my compositions originated in the bathroom. I have rarely had a case of writer's block that a long, hot shower couldn't cure. This daily ritual is a chance for me to let my mind go free, to catch and reflect over any thoughts that drift through my head before they vanish like the ephemeral flashes of fireflies. I stand with my eyes closed, water running through my dripping hair, and try to derive the full meaning conveyed in chapter six of my favorite book, *Zen and the Art of Motorcycle Maintenance*. I'll be lathering shampoo into the mass of tangles that is my hair as I work on a synaesthesia for the next two lines of a poem, or the conditioner will be slowly soaking through when I experience an Archimedean high, as a hard-to-grasp physics concept presented earlier in the day suddenly reveals itself to me. Now, if only they had let me take that AP Calculus test in the shower . . .

The sparkles of falling water mesmerize me into reflection. Thoughts tumbling in somersaults soften into a dewy mellowness. Do these drops of water carry a seed of consciousness within them? As I watch the water winking with the reflected light of the bathroom, it appears to glow in the fulfillment of its karma. Then, for a split second, all thoughts cease to exist and time stands still in a moment of perfect silence and calm like the mirror surface of a placid lake.

I know I have a tendency to deplete the house supply of hot water, much to the annoyance of the rest of my family. I know I should heed my mother's continual warnings of the disastrous state of my skin after years of these long showers; as it is, I go through two bottles of lotion a month to cure my post-shower "prune" syndrome. But my shower is too important to me. It is a small pocket of time away from the frantic deadline and countless places to be and things to do. It is a chance to reflect, and enjoy—a bit of welcome friction to slow down a hectic day. The water flows into a swirling spiral down the drain beneath my feet. It cleanses not only my body, but my mind and soul, leaving the bare essence that is me.

ANALYSIS

This essay illustrates how something as ordinary as a hot shower can be used auspiciously to reveal anything of the author's choosing. Mahajan could have focused on the academic subjects or extracurriculars she mentions in her essay, such as physics or the Rape Crisis Team, but instead she chooses a daily ritual common to us all. Though everyone can relate to taking a shower, doubtless few shower in quite the same way Mahajan does or find it to be such an intellectually and emotionally stirring experience. The intimacy of the act sets an appropriate stage for her personal description of unraveling from life's stresses by singing into a shampoo bottle microphone.

There is no single, clear focus to the essay, but this accurately reflects the shower experience itself—"to catch and reflect over any thoughts that drift through my head before they vanish." Mahajan touches on schoolwork, classical Indian music and contemplation about her favorite book, all with humorous flair, and she even goes into emotionally revealing descriptions of crying in the shower. Unfortunately, she dwells on crying for an entire paragraph, and the reader cannot help but wonder whether she could survive without her shower to cleanse her "mind and soul." Ultimately, that Mahajan derives literally so much inspiration and relief from the shower seems rather hard to believe. The notion that she could have done better on her AP Calculus test had she been allowed to take it in the shower is amusing, but doesn't seem to add much beyond the suggestion that she is dependent upon these showers. And that she finally did understand that vague "hard-to-grasp physics concept" seems excessive. Already she distinctly conveys her interest in science through her language—"the perfect coefficient of absorption for repeated reflections of sound waves"—and a supposedly subtle reaffirmation of this interest seems unnecessary.

Mahajan's vivid language and unusual descriptions are principle qualities of this essay. She deftly avoids the temptation of resorting to clichés, and most everything is entirely unpredictable. A relatively minor point is that her economy of language could be improved, as otherwise fluid sentences are occasionally overdone with an excess of adjectives and adverbs. Nonetheless, Mahajan conveys her talent for creative writing, and this carries her essay far beyond the lesser issues mentioned earlier. And, of course, her distinctive shower theme helps this exhibition of talent stand out.

—Ronald Y. Koo

"To Tell a Story"

By Ashley Evans, who attended a small private school in
Greenwich, Connecticut.

I can't remember not wanting to be a writer. I can't remember the
moment that, when I was five or six or seven, must have come, when
I discovered what had always been true: people made the worlds in
books, worlds I loved, and I wanted to be one of those people. And so
I read—in the bathtub, the car, a favorite tree. At night, characters
floated through my dreams, and by day, they waited, watching, just
beyond the periphery of my sight.

As surely as I knew that I wanted to write, it took a rainy midwinter
evening to teach me why. I was ten, sitting at the kitchen table set for
dinner, and I was reading; my mother stood cooking at the stove. I
looked up—her face had the distance and distraction of one about to
cry.

I had seen that face often in recent weeks: my mother's father had
just died. When she would reach a moment of pause—watching a
traffic light remain stubbornly red, hearing silence conquer laughter—
some command from within would draw her face away from me, the
present, and the world which now lacked one so dear. I asked her, that
day, what was wrong, and her mouth almost smiled, her face almost
came back to me as she told of the pork chops she would make with
her father when her mother went out. She told me about the seasonings
he let her choose with baby hands, about the smell that rose from the
pan, and about his professed delight at any taste.

She told me these things, and, after she spoke, tears flowed along
her cheeks, fell from her chin, and exploded in the pan. We laughed,
she cried, and then, once again, we laughed. I looked at my mother,
and in the egotism of childhood I could not imagine that she would
one day be buried, and that buried with her bones would be her un-

uttered thoughts, her unrealized dreams. I felt sorry for her, my mother, and I grew angry with the thought of myself standing over a stove, having to explain to a child how pork chops can make a grown woman cry. I resented my books, then, and the stories they told of other peoples' lives, and that resentment—fueled, I believe now, with envy— taught me why I wanted to be a writer.

I would tell my own stories, I decided that night as my mother's tears fell with the ease of the rain, and I would teach the truest of my thoughts, the core of myself, to find expression on the page I want to get as many perspectives on this life as I can, educate myself in as many disciplines as my capabilities permit, defer to wiser authorities on territories that have been charted, so that, in the end, I might tell my own story. I want to try to discover what it is, truly, to be human, and some voice, whispering in tones too quiet to be clear, tells me that writing is my way.

ANALYSIS

Evans's choice of topic is bold, since it invites an assessment of her ability as a writer. Yet she makes it easy to approve of her ambitions, presenting an essay that is both affecting and propulsive. By lending her own voice to her mother's memories, she adds a layer of narrative complexity most college essays lack. Complexity here, however, does not mean a loss of clarity. Excellent turns of phrase and skillfully selected observations keep Evans's discussion of death from being cumbersome and clichéd.

It is a good idea to explain your dreams as well as describe them. Evans's intelligent prose makes the process seem effortless, but far from thoughtless. College applicants may also want to consider her approach to writing about the death of a relative in order to strike the right note of emotional authenticity.

—Matthew A. Carter

"A Grateful Glance into Trash"

By David Soloveichik, who attended a small private high school in
Los Angeles, California.

I spent hours staring at trash. Often, rather than going home, playing games outside with other four-year-olds, or watching cartoons, I insisted that my grandmother take me to the local rubbish dump. I was still in Kiev then, and piles of technological trash were quite common. There were remnants of bicycles, old television sets, broken cameras, pieces of mystical electronic equipment, cylinders, and other parts of internal combustion engines, all intriguing and exciting. A cylinder's head, still almost shiny, looked like a leg of a robot. What purpose did this metallic curiosity fulfill? Why was it made and then thrown into this pile of rusting, crumbling, variegated junk? This was a puzzle, a mechanical system with knowns and unknowns where I could always find a solution if I looked deeply enough. My mother warned me that if I kept wasting my time, I would grow up to be a garbageman. I told her that that's exactly what I wanted to become. She didn't understand that amid tires, cables, refrigerators, gyros, labels, and carburetors I found interest, imagination, and logical thought.

The garbage dump was the first arena of my intellectual upbringing. From then on my curiosity has always found something new, undiscovered, and fascinating. This curiosity leads me through life, from gears to automatic transmissions, from light bulbs to lasers. It guides me under strangers' cars and into construction zones. When my family and I immigrated to the U.S., it led me to stare, amazed, at automatic doors and supermarket scanners. However, the first time my curiosity was truly sparked was among those glistening metallic pieces of trash. Garbage trucks or lymphocytes, automatic doors or membrane channel proteins, cylinders or ATP pumps—from then on my world was always full of working little parts that could be understood, dissected, and logically analyzed.

I am now seventeen and pursuing my research, not at a garbage dump, but at the equipped laboratories of the high school, the computer at home, and this summer at the UCLA biotechnology laboratory. The logical connections I now make are between mathematical theorems, physical principles, and program functions. I dissect pieces of DNA using restriction enzymes and use light to analyze the chemical composition of stars. But I still like, from time to time, to take a grateful glance into trash: the evidence of society's creativity and ingenuity. One never knows what inspiration can be found there.

ANALYSIS

With elegant understatement, this author turns a childhood fascination with garbage into a well-polished, sophisticated essay. Employing vivid description and concise prose, the author captures the raw emotion of a child's curiosity and uses it to highlight both his intellectual and individual growth. In doing so, his work proves that a successful essay need not tackle the meaning of life or challenge a widely held ideal in order to carry significant weight with a reader. Even within the bounds of the relatively brief three-paragraph piece, this author is able to detail a number of very personal experiences—his upbringing, immigration to the United States and intellectual awakening—all under the guise of garbage.

From the first sentence, the author is particularly successful at drawing the reader in and keeping his or her attention through the entire piece. The image of the author as child, staring at trash, creates an immediate sense of tension and forces the reader to ponder why this is in fact the case. But the writer does not let up, and uses direct questions to force the reader to stay an active participant in the narrative. By the same token, the opening sentence of the essay's middle paragraph provides an effective and intriguing transition that helps reinforce the essay's well-established sense of flow.

Despite the overall strength of the work, however, the author puts a slight damper on his piece with a less-than-impressive final sentence. Although in the second to last sentence the author skillfully brings the reader full circle to the essay's opening point, his conclusion loses steam. By simply removing the last sentence, the essay could end on a strong and elegant note.

—Scott A. Resnick

"Ginsberg"

By Sasha Haines-Stiles, who attended a small private day school in rural Martinsville, New Jersey.

I remember vividly third grade English class: writing furiously with a thick pencil and a colored rubber grip. I loved to fill up blank sheets of paper, to read my stories out loud and see that I had my classmates' attention.

As I and my appreciation for words grew, I became fascinated by poetry. I read the collected works of Allen Ginsberg, Anne Sexton, T. S. Eliot and Walt Whitman, and soon I began to write verse myself. Though I was secretly proud of my work, I wasn't sure that anyone else would like my poetry. Even after I was convinced by teachers to write for the school literary magazine and won first place in a creative writing contest, I displayed my work in public hesitatingly. Then something happened that changed all that.

A friend of mine met Allen Ginsberg at a poetry reading two years ago, and Ginsberg invited him to "drop by" his apartment in New York some time. My friend, knowing that I had a "thing" for Ginsberg's writing, took him up on his offer—and brought me along. I, in turn, brought along my poetry. I doubted that Ginsberg would want to read it, but I fully intended to at least ask him to do so. I desperately wanted to hear what the most famous figure in contemporary poetry had to say about my work. (Not that I hadn't already fantasized the perfect dialogue . . .)

When my friend and I arrived at his apartment, and he opened the door and ushered us into his hallway, I couldn't believe it was Allen Ginsberg shaking my hand, touching my shoulder, guiding me into the kitchen. "Have some of this mushroom omelet I just made," he said. "Let me play a tape for you. It's a musical version of a poem of mine. Paul McCartney just mixed it and sent it over and no one else has heard it yet. Do you like these sketches I've been working on? Make some tea for yourselves!" We did, and then sat around the kitchen table sipping our tea and chatting like old friends. Finally, I gathered my courage and handed him my papers.

As he read the first poem, I studied intently the grain of the wood of his kitchen table. Then I looked up so I could watch him, gauge his reaction. He made notes in the margins, laughed out loud at certain parts, mumbled, "good, wonderful phrase, perfect work. Hmm." He raised his eyes and peered at me over the top of his glasses. "Sasha," he said, "do you see why I'd change this? Let me explain . . ."

When it was time for us to go, Ginsberg walked with us down to the street. At the corner, as we waited for the light to change, he put his mouth to my ear and whispered, "You have a way with words." He kissed me on the cheek and held my hands in his and smiled. The light turned red for the cars; he waved goodbye as we crossed the street.

Months later, I took the stage at open mike at the Dodge Poetry Festival. With a steady gaze, a self-assured smile and revised poems in hand, I heard my voice over the sound system, heard my words amplified echoing. I heard the wild applause and whistles and catcalls and remembered my idol, my mentor, Allen Ginsberg telling me, "Nice words here, this is really quite good." I believed him.

ANALYSIS

In this essay, the applicant describes a confidence-building moment as the result of an encounter with the famous contemporary poet, Allen Ginsburg. The applicant explains that she has been interested in writing and reading poetry since an early age, but has often questioned whether or not others would appreciate her work. Her conversation with Ginsberg gave her the confidence to feel more comfortable with writing. This is a wonderful topic to write about for a number of reasons. It involves an experience of which many aspiring poets can only dream and demonstrates a moment of personal growth. Also, this highly unique experience is able to be adequately summarized in a relatively short amount of space.

Beside the unique nature of the topic, the other strength of this essay is that the reader can learn a great deal about the applicant. On the one hand, the fact that the applicant is often nervous about what people think about her writing signals that she is probably modest. This humility allows her to inform the reader that she wrote for her high school literary magazine and that she won first place in a creative writing contest. Usually, such explicit references to accomplishments in the essay often make the applicant seem arrogant; however, this is not the case here due to the perceived modesty of the author. This information also serves as an objective testament to her poetry writing skills. The applicant's use of dialogue and direct quotations to describe her encounter with Ginsberg is also an interesting way of describing her encounter—it adds to the realism of her telling of the story. Oftentimes, applicants are too general when attempting to describe a specific experience or situation—it's often difficult for the reader to get a picture of the event in his/her mind. The use of dialogue helps to avoid this pitfall; it gives the reader a more in-depth perspective. Overall, the essay ties together nicely and is very focused on how a specific event can shape the applicant's life.

One area of improvement could be for the applicant to add more description to her encounter with Ginsburg. While the dialogue is engaging it would have been interesting to have more of a physical description of Ginsburg and his apartment, giving the reader a more vivid description of the meeting.

—Joshua H. Simon

SONGS OF EXPERIENCE

"Should I Jump?"

By Timothy F. Sohn, who attended a medium-sized public high school in Tarrytown, New York.

As I stood atop the old railroad-bridge some six stories above the water, my mind was racing down convoluted paths of thought: Logic and reason would oblige me to get off this rusting trestle, run to my car, fasten my seat belt, and drive home carefully while obeying the speed limit and stopping for any animals which might wander into my path. This banal and utterly safe scenario did not sit well with me. I felt the need to do something reckless and impetuous.

"Why am I doing this?"

I backed up to where I could no longer see the huge drop which awaited me, and then, my whole body trembling with anticipation, I ran up to the edge, and hurled myself off the bridge.

"Do I have a death wish? Will my next conversation be with Elvis or Jimmy Hoffa?"

The first jump off the bridge was like nothing I had ever experienced. I do not have a fascination with death, and I do not display suicidal tendencies, yet I loved throwing myself off that bridge, despite the objections of the logical part of my brain. Standing up there, I recalled from physics that I would be pulled toward the earth with an acceleration of 9.8m/s/s. G-forces meant nothing to me once I stepped off the edge of the bridge, though. I felt like I was in the air for an eternity (although I was actually only in the air for about three seconds).

This leap was at once the most frightening and most exhilarating experience of my life. That synergy of fear and excitement brought about a unique kind of euphoria. Jumping off and feeling the ground fall out from underneath me was incredible. I have rock-climbed and rappelled extensively, but those experiences cannot compare, either in fear or in thrill, to jumping off a bridge.

Once I conquered my initial fear and jumped off, I did it again and again, always searching for that tingling sensation which ran through my limbs the first time I did it, but never quite recapturing the astonishing bliss of that first jump. I have jumped many times since that first time, and all of my jumps have been fun, but none can quite match that first leap. The thrill of that first jump, that elusive rapture, was one of the greatest feelings of my life.

"Wow, I can't believe I did that!"

When I jumped off that bridge, I was having fun, but I was also rebelling. I was making amends for every time I did the logical thing instead of the fun thing, every time I opted for the least dangerous route throughout my life. I was rising up and doing something blissfully bad, something impetuous. I was acting without thinking of the ramifications, and it was liberating. My whole life, it seemed, had been lived within the constrictive boundaries of logical thought. I overstepped those boundaries when I jumped. I freed myself from the bonds of logic and reason, if for only a few seconds, and that was important.

ANALYSIS

In this essay, Sohn presents a captivating narrative of an experience that has significantly shaped his attitudes and outlook on life. In order for this narrative form to be successful, the writer must use descriptive language to set the scene and transport the reader to the location and even into the thought process of the narrator. Sohn does this remarkably well. The reader can envision the railroad trestle upon which he stands and even feel the weightlessness of his free-fall thanks to clear, descriptive language. Sohn uses a mature vocabulary and incorporates an internal dialogue to aid the flow of his essay successfully.

The inevitable goal of such a format is for the writer to convey something about his or her personality or individual qualities to the reader. In this case, Sohn wanted the reader to know about his freewheeling side; his ability to take risks, defy logic, and experience danger. The conclusion is also a particular strength of this essay. Sohn takes the isolated event he has described so well and applies it to a broader scheme, showing the reader just how this event was truly significant to his life.

—Adam S. Cohen

"History"

By Daniel Droller, who attended a small public high school in
Pelham, New York.

The day had been going slowly. On other days I had been more
successful in my research on the connection between Switzerland
and Nazi gold. However, today I hadn't found anything substantial yet.
I couldn't stop myself from looking at my watch to see if a time had
come when I could take the shuttle back to Washington. Josh, the other
intern, had been luckier. He had found a new piece of information
dealing with Herman Goering. Like other information we had uncovered at the National Archives II, it could be extremely important for
the Senate Banking Committee, or just a widely known fact with which
we would be wasting our supervisor's time. At any rate, he flagged it
for copying and kept on searching his box.

I finished my box of files, checked my watch again, and decided
that I could search through one more box before I had to take the hour-
long bus ride back. The group of records on the next cart was marked
"Top Secret Intercepted Messages from the U.S. Military Attache in
Berne, Switzerland, to the War Department in Washington D.C." Following the Archives' procedures, I took one box off of the cart, then
one folder out of the box, put the box in the middle of the table, and
started looking through documents in the folder.

In this folder there was one document that caught my eye. It was
dated "23 February 1945" and contained information sent to Washington on bombings of the previous day. Many of the documents I had
gone through had recounted battles and bombings as well as the areas
affected by these. What was different about this document was that the
cities listed as being bombed were Swiss cities. This was very strange
because Switzerland was a neutral country and its cities shouldn't have
been bombed. I recognized the names of many of the cities that were

mentioned in the message, since I had gone to visit these when I had visited my mother's family in Switzerland. They were listed as follows:

B-17's. Fighters at 1240 machine-gunned military post near Lohn north of Scahffhausen. 3 wounded.
At 1235 Stein on Rhine bombed. 7 dead. 16 wounded. 3 children missing.

About halfway through the list I saw the following:

At 1345 B-17's bombed Rafz. 8 dead, houses destroyed.

I was shocked. My mother is from Rafz, and most of her family still lives there. Even more disturbing was the date of the message. My mother would have been only four years old.

"Josh, you'll never guess what I just found! The town where my Mom grew up was bombed. She was . . . four years old! This is so weird!"

"Yeah, that is pretty weird." Obviously, Josh wasn't as enthusiastic as I was.

I stayed until the last shuttle at 6:00 to go through the rest of the boxes on the cart, but didn't find anything nearly as good. I really couldn't believe it, my Mom had never mentioned anything about a bombing, and I assumed that she didn't remember it. This made me even more excited because I had uncovered a piece of my history. I couldn't wait to call home that night.

When I got to the dorm, I said "hi" to a few of the ballerinas and other interns I had met that summer, and ran up to my room. As soon as I got in, I picked up the phone and called home.

"Yallo?"

"Hey, Moms!"

"Hi, Daniel. How was work? Did you find anything for Alfonse?"

"Not really, Moms, but . . ."

"How are the ballerinas?"

"Fine, but Moms. Listen. What do you remember about February 22, 1945"

There was slight hesitation on her end of the line. It was only for a few seconds, but I thought that I had stumped her. She was only four years old at the time of the bombing; she shouldn't remember. But in a few seconds she spoke. The jovial manner of before had been replaced by one solemnity. She had remembered.

"That was the day the Americans bombed Rafz."

ANALYSIS

"History" is about the discovery of one's past. Droller describes his findings of a small, yet significant, piece of history concerning his mother. The reader is not given a complete picture of the applicant's background. Instead, the essay succeeds in revealing one personal and meaningful moment in Droller's life that would otherwise not have been captured by the rest of his application.

Through his essay, Droller describes how he accidentally came across a part of his history. What most stands out is the shock and surprise that he feels with his newfound information. While Droller does tell us outright about his excitement, "I had uncovered a piece of my history," he also illustrates his enthusiasm with the description of his telephone conversation and his impatience to reveal his findings. This leaves the reader wanting to learn more about the details of the bombing and how it affected his family.

The essay's form could, however, be made stronger. Despite the defining moment found at the very end of the essay, the opening has little direction. There isn't much indication as to the main point of the essay. A reader would probably be more interested in the details surrounding the bombing, shedding more light on the relationship between mother and son. We are not shown how this discovery affected their relationship or if Droller now thinks differently about his mother based on what she went through during her childhood. A detailed account of the author's interactions with his mother, and his knowledge of his mother's childhood, might have made the final realization about the bombing more emotional and revealing about Droller's character.

—Daniel A. Shapiro

"To Soar, Free"

By Vanessa G. Henke, of Riverdale, New York, who attended a mid-size public magnet school in New York City.

A cold, blustery winter storm swept my grandparents and I into the warmth of my aunt's living room, where she was hosting her traditional Christmas Eve party. My hat and cape were taken from me, revealing the Victorian party dress, which had been designed and painstakingly tailored just for me. The music lifted me, and chills surged through my body. I was enthralled, ecstatic with the power of the orchestra. My excitement mounted as I realized that, for a few brief moments, the audience at the opening night of *The Nutcracker* at New York City's Lincoln Center was focusing on my performance. At nine years old, this was my long-awaited debut. Any vestige of uncertainty about my performance had dissipated. I was transformed from a shy young girl into a confident performer.

Over the years, as my technique improved and I spent increasing amounts of time each week practicing and performing, I learned to value the discipline required of a professional. Without so many hours dedicated to practice, I would never have been able to execute powerful leaps across the stage in performance. In class, or on stage, the music would pulse through every fiber of my being, my body resonating to every note of the score. I discovered that discipline and dedication gave me the confidence necessary for me to refine my technique and style, and to fulfill my potential and dream—to dance like another instrument in the orchestra.

This past summer, I taught ballet and choreographed dance at Buck's Rock Camp for the Creative and Performing Arts. There, I discovered that fulfillment can come not only from soaring across the stage, but by communicating what I have learned to others. I emulated the good techniques of my best teachers, so that my students could find pleasure in dance. For my more advanced students, I offered well-deserved praise and helped them to refine their skills. For students with less experience, I tried to foster self-confidence and create an environment in which they could learn, ask questions and make mistakes without feeling ashamed. The rewards for my efforts were the students' improved self-confidence and skills.

The discipline I learned during my five years with the New York City Ballet helped me understand that with freedom comes responsibility. When I performed at Lincoln Center, I danced across the stage, free, because of the hours of preparation and thoughtful consideration I put into planning classes and rehearsals, inspiring students to be their best. I now have a greater appreciation for the value of my experiences as a performer, I am a more fulfilled person and I feel confident and enthusiastic about future endeavors. I will continue to soar, free.

ANALYSIS

In her essay, the author of "To Soar, Free" demonstrates an understanding that if an essay about a "significant experience or achievement" is to be successful, it must distinguish itself from a pack of surely similar essay topics. Although the author's chosen topic is not all that different than writing about playing sports or performing other types of art, this essay stands out. The author gracefully highlights the personal importance of performing and teaching ballet, using her progression in the art to reflect her personal and physical growth. Beginning with a childhood memory about her first ballet performance, the author begins to paint a picture for the reader of just how dance has influenced her life. From there, the reader gets a sense of the increasing significance of this activity, to the point where he or she learns that this love for ballet has inspired the author to instruct others in her art form. In her final paragraph, the essayist closes with general conclusions about the lessons she has learned through dance.

By beginning her passage with an anecdote about her first major ballet performance, the author distances her piece from a more straightforward "what-dancing-means-to-me" essay. Instead of spelling out the reasoning behind her love of ballet, the author encourages the reader to continue reading. Not until the end of the fourth sentence does he or she know what exactly has been causing the chills and excitement that the author illustrates so well in the opening sentences. With a setting firmly established, the author is then free to proceed with her narrative. The reader observes the author's love of dance grew more intense as she got older and became more serious about this activity. Moreover, in the third paragraph, the author introduces an interesting twist to the essay, as she chronicles her experiences on the other side of dance, as a ballet teacher at a summer camp. This complication works well at illuminating the way in which the author learns to see that ballet can offer more fulfillment than just that from the thrill of performance.

Although this essay is effective at highlighting the many ways in which ballet has affected the author's life, it lacks flow and does not efficiently link its varied points and ideas. The connection between the second and third paragraphs is especially abrupt. This spot is an ideal juncture to suggest the many ways in which dance—aside from its direct performance and practice—has influenced her life. Especially in essays about significant personal experiences or achievements, it is extremely important to make effective use of transitional phrases and words to connect the individual points with the overall theme. Be that as it may, after compiling a solid essay with unique perspectives and dimensions, the author subtracts from her piece by offering clichéd conclusions in the final paragraph that are easy to incorporate into any essay of this form. The challenge is to identify and highlight conclusions unique to the situation.

—Scott A. Resnick

"One Hundred Pairs of Eyes"

By Patricia M. Glynn, who attended a public high school in rural
Plymouth, Massachusetts.

Awareness. An awareness that all eyes from one hundred yards of
green grass are focused on a certain point in space is what drives
through my thoughts as I stand poised. These eyes disregard the pe-
ripheral chatter of spectators, the cold wind whistling in the night air
around them, and the harshness of the white lights over the field. They
focus only on this one spot before my hands and, to begin their show,
they wait for a simple motion, a mere flick of the wrist. As a tingling
sensation arises in my fingertips, I lift my hands in preparation. One
hundred pairs of eyes breathe in unison across the hundred yards, and
my hands descend in a practiced pattern toward that one point in
space. It is that point where the hundred pairs of eyes release their
breath into their various instruments, where the music is created, and
where the show begins.

This experience is one that I get to relive every Friday night while
conducting the Plymouth High School marching band in its weekly
half-time performance for the football fans. While I have performed as
one of the pairs of eyes, as conductor and Senior Drum major I feel a
greater part of the show than I ever did before. I feel every note and
every phrase of music from every instrument, and I pull even more
music from those instruments. Their intensity is sparked from my intensity, and mine builds on theirs. The intensity is not only from the
music; it comes from the eyes. It's my eyes scanning the field, scouting
for problems, and brokering confidence that command an intensity in
response. This is the greatest feeling in the world.

As my motions become larger and larger and my left hand pushes
upward, I demand volume from the band while it crescendos toward
its final notes. Building volume and drive, this music sends a tingling

sensation from my fingertips through my wrists and pulsing through my body. My shoulders ache but keep driving the beat, and my emotions are keyed up. As the brass builds and the band snaps to attention in the last picture of the show, the percussion line pushes the music with a driving hit. Musicians and conductor alike climax with the music until reaching that same instant in time. With a rigorous closing of my fists, the music stops, but the eyes hold their focus, instruments poised, until a smile stretches across my face and my features relax, tingling with pent up emotion. Applause.

ANALYSIS

An essay that asks for discussion of an important extracurricular activity may be just the place for an applicant to discuss in greater detail why participating in student government makes his or her world go 'round. But as in this case, the essay may also offer an opportunity for an applicant to further describe a unique or unconventional interest. "One Hundred Pairs of Eyes" details the author's experiences as conductor of her high school football band—a position that on paper may not carry much weight, despite its many responsibilities. Through her description of leading one hundred musicians in the complexities of a half-time show, the reader gains unique insight into being at the helm of a marching band—a position from which few people have observed the perspective.

The author begins her essays with rich description—she is the point of focus for one hundred sets of eyes. By personifying the eyes, the author paints a marvelous picture of the scene. The reader can almost sense the position from which she must be standing and the enormity of the group at her feet. But he or she is left to wonder what sort of awkward situation may be causing this unique scenario. Just as the author creates an intense sensation of tension in the essay, the reader too holds his or her breath in advance of the announcement that Glynn is the leader of a marching band. As she continues, the author contrasts her experiences as conductor with those of being a performer, shedding light on the exhilaration of holding the gaze of the hundred musicians who look to her for rhythm and tempo. And with descriptive language in the third paragraph, the author encourages the reader to push onward, toward the finale of both the music and the essay. The passage ends with an impressive sense of relief both for the band members and the reader.

—Scott A. Resnick

"The Lost Game"

By Stephanie A. Stuart, who attended a small college-preparatory high school in Monterey, California.

When I was little my father used to play a game with me driving home. Its main substance was something like this: he would say, oh no, I seem to be lost; how shall we get home? And then he would ask, which way? Gleefully, I would crane my neck above the seat; according to the game, his befuddlement was hopeless, and I alone as navigator could bring us home. No doubt I seemed contrary as I directed him further and further down back streets, but my secret incentive was exploration. As a small child there is very little one can control in one's world; to have control over an entire grown-up—not to mention a whole car—was tremendously appealing. The real allure, though, was in going the "wrong" way—as soon as we turned left where we usually turned right, the world was so brand new it might have only appeared the moment we rounded the corner. My heart would beat below my throat as I gave the direction to turn, stretching my neck from my place in the backseat, eager and afraid: Suppose I did really get us lost? The secret desire to discover always won out over the fear, but I can still recall the flutter of my heart on the inside of my ribs as I navigated the roundabout connections which was as mysterious as the Northwest Passage, lone link between the cul-de-sacs.

Exploration was a quest I took to heart; alone, I would set out on expeditions into our back yard, or down the street, creating a mental map concentric to our doorstep. Discovery bloomed magical for me; marked on the map were the locations of abandoned tree houses, bell-blue flowers and plants with flat powdery leaves the size of silver dollars.

The other night it fell to my brother and me to return a movie. After we left it on the counter, though, our sense of adventure got the better of us. Oh dear, I said, I seemed to be lost. Where shall I go? Eager to discover the town which smoldered at one o'clock under the orange and violet of sodium street lamps, he chose the road less traveled, at least by our wheels.

We wound into the pine forest in the dead of night; moonlight feel eerie across our laps, striated by tree trunks. I crested a hill slowly: Monterey spread in a lighted grid below us, down to the darkening sea.

Above, the Milky Way sprang apart and arched like a dance. I angled my ear for a moment to Gatsby's tuning fork, that pure, enticing tone that echoes from the spheres. Think, remember, I wished upon him, what it is to explore, and the explorer's incentive: discovery.

"Which way?" I asked him, and he grinned slowly, moonlight glinting far-off mischief in his eyes. The streets spread orthogonal before us; the pure realm of possibility opened from them.

"Straight ahead," he said, and I smiled.

ANALYSIS

Stephanie's essay falls into the life experiences category. However, rather than focusing on a single life-changing experience, Stephanie shows her approach toward personal discovery by relating the story of riding in a car and changing the standard directions as a means of stumbling upon unexplored worlds. The essay is well controlled—at no point does she stray toward overstating the significance of these individual events, but deftly uses them as a tool to illustrate her adventure-seeking attitude toward life and her unwillingness to be satisfied with the routine. Stephanie further highlighted the importance of discovery when she submitted the essay to the admissions office on U.S. Geological Survey maps—a thoughtful touch.

The essay's greatest asset is the sense of personal development Stephanie conveys. What begins as a cute story of her childhood is used wonderfully to highlight her personal development as she writes of a tenet in her life: "Think, remember . . . what it is to explore, and the explorer's incentive: discovery." Stephanie avoids listing her accomplishments in a résumé put into sentence form, but still captures important aspects of her identity, namely her inquisitiveness. The essay is well-paced and calm, with a solid development from beginning to end. Stephanie describes sensory aspects of her story ("flat, powdery leaves the size of silver dollars") with great word choice without overdoing it. It is clear that every word in the essay was carefully chosen to accurately and succinctly describe her subject. Not only does her essay successfully paint a picture of her as an curious little child, it shows that the same inquisitiveness she exhibited then she still possesses, now coupled with more responsibility, as she drives her brother and encourages his inquisitiveness.

The biggest risk in this essay is that it does not adequately showcase her accomplishments, normally a standard part of a college essay. While it worked for her, this has much to do with the extraordinary level of care she took in crafting the essay; her diligence shows, and the essay is an insightful, well-written, and well-paced piece of work.

—Jason M. Goins

"Warm Hearts and a Cold Gun"

By James A. Colbert, who attended a medium-sized private boarding school in Deerfield, Massachusetts.

If a six-foot-tall man slinging a semi-automatic rifle had approached me in Greenfield, I probably would have screamed for help. However, being in a foreign land, unable even to speak the native tongue, my options of recourse were significantly limited. The looming creature, dressed mostly in black, with short, dark hair, proceeded to grasp my right hand. As a smile furtively crept across his face, he mouthed, "Time to get on the bus."

"What?" I nervously spurted at the cold weapon before me.

"I'm sorry. I didn't introduce myself," he said. "I'm Ofir, your counselor."

Completely unnerved, I hurried onto the bus to be sure the gun remained at his side. "Did you know one of our leaders is a guy with a gun?" I asked a girl from Philadelphia, sitting beside me.

"What did you expect? This is Israel, not New England."

At the end of my junior year I decided to go to Israel to escape from the stimulating but confining atmosphere of Deerfield Academy. I yearned for a new environment where I could meet students unlike the ones I knew, where I could explore a foreign culture, and where I could learn more about my religion. The brochure from the Nesiya Institute had mentioned a "creative journey" featuring hikes in the desert, workshops with prominent Israeli artists, dialogues between Arabs and Jews, and discussions on Israeli culture and Judaism, but nowhere had it mentioned counselors with rifles. I suddenly wondered if I had made the right decision.

Weeks later, sitting outside the Bayit Va'gan Youth Hostel as the sun began to sink in the Israeli sky, I smiled with reassurance. As I looked up from writing in my journal, a group of misty clouds converged to form an opaque mass. But the inexorable sun demonstrated her tenacity. One by one, golden arrows pierced the celestial canopy to illuminate the lush, green valley between Yad Vashem and the hills of western Jerusalem. I could feel holiness in those rays of golden light that radiated from the sun like spokes of a heavenly wheel.

That moment was one of the most spiritual of my life. The natural grandeur of the sight seemed to bring together the most meaningful experiences of my five weeks in Israel: watching the sunrise over the Red Sea, wading chest-deep through a stream in the Golan Heights, looking up at the myriad stars in the desert sky, exploring a cave in Negev, and climbing the limestone precipice of Masada. These natural temples far surpassed any limestone sanctuary built by man.

Shifting my gaze downwards, I noticed Ofir standing beside me with his eyes fixed on the sacred valley. At age twenty-five, his head was already balding, but the expression on his face, with his eyes stretched wide and his jaws parted, reminded me of a child starting with delight at a fish in an aquarium. For over a minute neither of us spoke. That poignant silence said more than a thousand words could ever express.

Being an empirical person, I need confirmation, to prove to myself that I understood.

Finally, I said to Ofir, "This is holiness." His weapon bounced as he swiveled to look me in the eye. As he nodded in affirmation, a beam of light transcended his pupils to produce a telling spark of corroboration.

Emerson said in "Nature," "The sun illuminates only the eye of man, but shines into the eye and heart of the child." I carried an L. L. Bean backpack, and Ofir carried an Uzi, but that afternoon as the sun warmed our hearts, we were both children.

ANALYSIS

The topic of this essay works well because it conveys the author's personal growth from an experience unique to most American students. His declaration of his decision to leave the atmosphere of his boarding school to travel abroad establishes him as a student willing to broaden his horizons and venture to the unknown. The initial comparison of Israel to his hometown is thoughtfully phrased and expresses his honest feelings.

The author is extremely concise in this essay, describing everything that is necessary and leaving out unnecessary details. His personal voice is evident. Rather than give plain descriptions of the places he visited, the author recalls his personal reaction to seeing such places, therefore allowing the reader to get to know the writer's own perspective.

The dialogue in this essay is also succinct, but complete. The author integrates other voices in his essay because those voices are part of his experience abroad. Finally, the closing quote from Emerson's "Nature" is well used and ties together with the poignant imagery of the contrasting L. L. Bean backpack and Uzi, leaving the reader with a vision of what the writer experienced.

—Nancy Poon

"In the Waiting Room"

By Carlin E. Wing, who attended a small private high school in Brooklyn, New York.

You will not think, my mind firmly informed me; you are much too busy being nervous to think. I sat in the mother of all waiting rooms. My pen traveled frantically across the pages of my black book, recording every detail of the room in fragments that passed for poetry. I tried to write something deeply insightful about the procedure I was about to undergo but failed to produce even an opening sentence. These were the final minutes before my hand would be separated from my pen for ten weeks. Even if I could not think, I needed to write. My eyes became my pen and I wrote:

Waiting Room
      the name dictates the atmosphere
The walls, papered in printed beige,
      are dotted with pastel pictures.
Two square columns interrupt the room,
      attended by brown plastic trash bins.
An undecided carpet of green, black, gray, red, blue
      mirrors the undecided feelings of the occupants.
And none of these mask the inevitable tension of the space.

I paused and lifted my head to stare at The Door that led to my fate.

My fate was to have wrist surgery. Three years before, I had been told that the fracture in my wrist would heal. Earlier this year, I was again sitting in front of X-rays and MRI results listening to the doctor say that the old fracture had been an indication that the ligaments and tendons were torn. I could have declined to have surgery and never played competitive squash again. It was never an option.

I am a jock. My competitive personality finds a safe place to release itself on a playing field. My strongest motivation is the prospect of doing what no one expects I can do. However, the hardest competition I face is that of my own expectations. Squash allows me to put the perfectionist in me to good use. The beauty of squash, and sports in general, is that I never reach an anti-climax because there is always a higher level to reach for. Squash requires a healthy wrist. Surgery would make my wrist healthy. My immediate reaction to the doctor's words was "Yes, I want surgery. How soon can it be done? How long until I can play squash again? Can I watch?"

No one understood that last part. My parents jokingly told their friends about my desire to observe the surgery, and the doctor was adamantly opposed to the idea. But I had not been joking. It was my wrist they were going to be working on. I thought that entitled me to watch. Anyhow, I had never seen an operation and was fascinated by the idea of someone being able to sew a tendon back together. I had this image of a doctor pulling out the needle and thread and setting to work, whistling. Perhaps subconsciously I wanted to supervise the operation, to make sure that all the little pieces were sewn back into the right places (admittedly not a very rational thought since I wouldn't know by sight if they were sewing them together or tearing them apart). I understood the doctor's fear that I would panic and mess up the operation. Still, I wanted to watch. I felt it would give me a degree of control over this injury that had come to dominate my life without permission. Unfortunately, the final decision was not mine to make and the surgery was to go unrecorded by my eyes, lost in the memories of doctors who perform these operations daily.

The Door opened and I looked up, tingling with hope and apprehension. In response to the nurse's call a fragile elderly lady in a cashmere sweater and flowered scarf was wheeled towards The Door by her son. As she passed me I overheard her say, "Let's rock and roll." The words echoed in my ears and penetrated my heart. As I watched her disappear beyond The Door, I silently thanked her for the sudden dose of courage she had unknowingly injected in me. If she could do it, I could do it. I was next and before too long I was lying on a gurney in a room filled with doctors. I told the anesthesiologist that I did not want to be put to sleep, even though a curtain hid the actual operation from my sight. I said "Hi" to Dr. Melone and, as the operation began, sang contentedly along with The Blues Brothers.

ANALYSIS

Chronicling an intimate moment or other personal experience requires particular attention and care in the essay-writing process. An author must be conscious that he or she creates an appropriate sense of balance that at once captures the reader while allowing for a sense of genuine personal reflection to show through. To be sure, the risk of turning the reader off with overly personal details or unnecessarily deep conclusions is a constant threat. However, "In the Waiting Room" reflects a successful attempt at convincing the reader that the author's wrist surgery merits his or her attention. Although unfocused, this work demonstrates that an essay about an otherwise insignificant topic can in fact be insightful and even touching.

By establishing a strong sense of tension at the beginning of the essay, "In the Waiting Room" succeeds where other personal reflection works often falter. The author does not begin with a topic sentence or other device that states the essay's point right away. To do so in this sort of essay would be to make the piece too much like a "what-I-did-last-summer" narrative. Instead, the reader is kept in suspense until the second paragraph of the piece of that which is causing the author's angst. Only then does the author spell out that it is his impending wrist surgery—and not a shot or test results—which has caused such great anxiety. As the essay continues, the author uses the occasion of waiting for the surgery to reflect on many of his complementary attributes: writer, athlete, coward and stoic. Overall, the writing is clear and unpretentious.

Yet in illustrating his multiple roles, the author tends to lose focus of the essay's overall point. Where it seems like the author portrays himself as an avid writer from the flow of the first paragraph, the reader is surprised to learn that the author is actually a self-described "jock" who plays squash. Before returning to the topic of the operation, the author takes another moment to reflect on his motivation for participating in sports. The essay loses significant steam and regains it only with the announcement that the author hopes to observe his own surgery. While interesting independently, these complications distract from the overall point. An essayist must be aware of the need to ensure that the flow of writing maintains a definite sense of direction—and doesn't meander too far from that path.

—Scott A. Resnick

"My Responsibility"

By David J. Bright, who attended a large public high school in
New York City.

When she hung up the phone, she immediately burst into tears and grabbed out in all directions for something to hold onto as she sank to the floor. I stood there motionless, not knowing what to do, not knowing what to say, not even knowing what had happened. It wasn't until I answered the door moments later and saw the police officers standing in the alcove that I finally discovered what had taken place. My fifteen-year-old brother had been arrested. It was only ten days before Christmas, a year ago today when it happened, but still I remember it like yesterday.

Robert had always been a rambunctious a child—wild and lively, as my mom always said. He was constantly joking around, playing pranks, and causing mayhem, but his engaging personality and small stature always seemed to save him from the firing line. This gave him the notion that he could cause any amount of trouble without feeling the repercussions. As a youngster growing up in Ireland, he had found few opportunities to get into a great deal of trouble. But four years ago at the age of twelve, the rules changed for him when he, my mother and I moved to America.

The same short stature that had been his ally in Ireland was now Robert's enemy in America. He was bullied and beaten on a daily basis. Since I couldn't be there all the time, Robert sought the protection from others. By the end of his first year in America, he had already joined a gang.

His appearance deteriorated, personality disappeared, and aggressiveness increased, leaving him an angry, hollowed out, manic depressive. After a year or so, his frighteningly self-destructive behavior and terrifying appearance forced my mom to send him to a suicide treatment center. There he received round the clock attention, counseling, and medication for his depression and aggressiveness. He was released after a couple of months.

Only a few short weeks later, supposedly after mixing his medication with alcohol, he went out with his friends to go to the store. There they robbed, shot, and killed a store clerk. Robert, as an accomplice to the crime, was charged with armed robbery and second degree murder.

Looking back now, I realize not what Robert had done wrong, but what I had done wrong. I had taken no interest in his welfare, and I never intervened when he needed me to. I just sat back and let it all come crashing down around me. It's in this respect that I guess I've changed the most. I'm now a much more involved person. I no longer allow things to just happen; I must be a part of everything that affects me. I'm also a more caring and better person. To make up for what I did—or rather, didn't do—I look out for those around me, my family and my friends. I act like a big brother to them to compensate for not being any kind of brother at all to Robert.

The experience hasn't only made me better. In a strange way, it was also the best thing that could have happened to Robert. He's turned his life around and is presently preparing to take the SATs in anticipation to go on to college, something the old Robert would never have done.

I guess it's sort of weird, isn't it. Such a dreadful experience can change an entire family's life, and how such a tragic situation could give birth to such great things.

ANALYSIS

Bright's intensely personal essay shows us the positive outcome of what seems like an overwhelmingly negative experience, that is, the arrest of his brother. Through his talkative, intimate writing style, Bright is able to reach his readers because he does not take a sentimental or moralistic tone. The strength of this essay lies in its honesty and its ability not only to criticize his brother, Robert, for his transgression, but to reprimand the author for his, as well. What makes this essay so unique is that Bright finds himself at fault and demonstrates his personal growth from his mistakes, unlike most college essays that are highly self-adulating in nature. Through accurately assessing where he went wrong by not acting like a true brother to Robert, Bright's piece is more impressive than most college essays.

Another great strength of Bright's essay is the maturity he displays by being able to take the blame for his brother's demise. This is a characteristic of a true big brother, one who knows how much his siblings admire and respect him, as well as value his judgment. Instead of harshly reproaching Robert for his crime, Bright turns to himself and how he "had taken no interest in his [Robert's] welfare." Furthermore, Bright illustrates how he was mature enough to learn from his errors and improve himself: "I act like a big brother . . . to compensate for not being any kind of brother at all to Robert." Bright is able to see that there are positive aspects of this bad experience and then applies them to his life; he shows to us that he is willing to change himself and make up for what he did not do for Robert by becoming "a much more involved person." In his essay, many aspects of Bright shine through: his maturity and strength, as well as his capacity to see a bright silver lining on what looks like a black thundercloud. Qualities such as these are ultimately the most important in terms of measuring who one is.

The only thing that Bright might have added to his essay is more of what happened to Robert. We learn that Robert was arrested, and is now studying for his SATs and preparing to go to college, but we are not told what happened to him between his arrest and his self-improvement. How did Robert decide to turn his life around? What challenges did he face? The second to last paragraph might need a little more detail as to how Robert went through the process of becoming who he is today. Yet, aside from this one minor comment, the essay stands on its own—it jumps out at the reader for its uniqueness, for its quiet, yet powerful, personal revelations.

—Marcelline Block

"The Line"

By Daniel B. Visel, who attended a small public high school in
Winnebago, Illinois.

There is no chance," wrote Ella Wheeler Wilcox, "no destiny, no
fate, that can circumvent or hinder or control the firm resolve of
a determined soul." These words are from her poem "Will," a favorite
of my Aunt May. Though Mrs. Wilcox's words on chance and destiny
never really caught my ear when Aunt May read it to me so many
times, those words resonated in my head December 9, 1994, a day that
I will never forget. On that day, I stood before Judge Stanley Pivner to
testify against my best friend, Wyatt.* The workings of fate are strange
indeed: Wyatt and I had been friends since kindergarten, when we
went to Suzuki violin lessons together. We had been the best of all
possible friends in grade school, helped each other through the troubled junior high years, and have remained close through high school.
Our paths, though, had led us in different directions: I spent all my
time studying for classes, while he invested time and money in souping
up his 1986 Dodge Ram. College didn't seem the necessity to him that
it did for me: Wyatt lived for the moment. The future, for him, would
be dealt with when he came to it.

Wyatt's crowd was a wild bunch. I was wary of them—they did
dangerous things. Somehow, I didn't associate Wyatt with any of this,
thought: he was Wyatt, my friend, a known quantity. I guess I had been
too busy studying to notice how much he had changed. It didn't hit me
until a Thursday night my senior year—the night that Wyatt pulled
up in his truck and asked if I was doing anything. I had finished my
math homework for the week, and had a good start on a draft of the

* not his real name

term paper I was writing on Dutch painters, so I said that I wasn't. I got in the truck with Wyatt, and we hit the road, heading to Barberton.

"Why are we going to Barberton?" I asked Wyatt.

"I got a plan," he replied, sounding dark. I noticed that there was a funny odor in the car—it smelled like beer. *Had Wyatt been drinking*? I wondered. I didn't say anything, though; I didn't want to lose face in front of someone I respected. There was a pained silence in the car as we sped towards Barberton. As I kept a firm eye on the road, making sure that Wyatt wasn't swerving or driving too fast, I recollected that Friday was the day of the Barberton football game.

We pulled up in the lot of the Barberton high school. I remained silent. To this day, I wonder why I didn't say something, why I couldn't find words to stop him. We got out of the truck; Wyatt got a pair of lockcutters out from under his seat, and I followed him around the back of the high school. You could puncture the silence with a stiletto.

I realized, too late, what was happening. Barberton was our high school rival; every year, people from our school talked about kidnapping the Barberton mascot, a male baboon named Heracles that they kept in a shed behind the school. Nobody actually did anything about it, though. Wyatt, though, seemed intent on changing that. I followed dumbly, my heart heavy with angst.

"Wyatt, this is lunacy," I told him. He said nothing, only smiled menacingly. I could smell the alcohol on his breath. I didn't know what to do; I followed his directions when he told me to stand guard. Quickly and skillfully he cut the lock holding the door shut, then opened the door. It was pitch-black inside the shed; Heracles was evidently asleep. He called out the beast's name; something stirred inside, there was a yawn, and Heracles came shambling out. I had never seen the monkey before; I was surprised at how friendly and well-mannered he was. He scrutinized us, looking for some kind of a handout I guess—how was he to know what Wyatt had in mind? Wyatt was impressed with Heracles's friendliness: he told me that this was going to be easier than we had thought. The monkey good-naturedly followed us back to the parking lot. With a little work, we succeeded in getting him into the back of the pickup truck. Wyatt threw a tarp over him, we got in the cab, and we started off, my brain full of anxiety.

Heracles, though, didn't seem to like the back of the truck that much. Somehow, he managed to get out from under the tarp; with a bound, he had jumped from the truck to the parking lot. Something tripped in Wyatt right then; to this day, I'm not sure what it was. I suspect it was the alcohol.

You have to draw the line somewhere. On that day, what started off as a simple high school prank went horribly wrong. It's important to support your friends, but there are some things that are simply not allowed—and running over a monkey with a pickup truck is one of them. Wyatt was out of control that night. Rage took hold of him: he was no longer my friend, he had sunk lower than the ape crushed beneath the wheels of his truck. And so, on a chilly day in December, I found myself on the witness stand, forced to bear witness against my best friend. Ella Wheeler Wilcox's words coursed through my blood that day: fate had taken the paths of our lives apart, but I was determined to do what was right. To follow the truth is a difficult path: it requires determination, a determination that I did not have the night we drove to Barberton. I learned something that night. It's a lesson that will stay with me my whole life.

ANALYSIS

Every application, just as every applicant, is unique. Everyone has a different story to tell. This applicant does a good job of telling the story of an experience that changed his life; although his story is a bit longer than is usual for an application, it is generally tight. The language is somewhat flowery: the number of superfluous adjectives and adverbs could be cut down. Some details might be thought of as extraneous. Nobody needs to know that the name of the mascot was Heracles, for example. However, such details as these put a human spin on the essay; the reader has an easy time constructing a mental picture of the applicant.

While this application has a strong story, the structure which brings it together is somewhat weak. The quote, while it may have deep personal significance to the author, seems like it could have been a random motivational quote grabbed off the Internet. Though the author tries hard to integrate it into the story, he never really succeeds; it seems, finally, irrelevant.

This essay shines in that it gives the reader an idea of some qualities that would not be brought out in the rest of the application. Loyalty, determination, and honor are not virtues that can be exhibited in a résumé. The author presents a difficult situation: torn between friendship and honesty, he chooses the latter. A few questions remain unanswered. Where is "Wyatt" now? Why does the author's resolution of principles take so long to come about? Nonetheless, Dan remains a poster boy for honesty, a virtue colleges are all too happy to rally behind.

—Maryanthe Malliaris

"Entering a Shaded World"

By Ezra S. Tessler, who attended a small private high school in
Philadelphia, Pennsylvania.

Bending my head to pass through the low doorway, I blinked deliberately, allowing my eyes to adjust to the dim light of the cav-
ernous room. Everything was a clouded dream, one that you are unable
to disentangle as it spins through your unconscious, but which somehow begins to unravel and become clearer only after you have awak-
ened. As my eyes adjusted to the darkness into which I had just
entered, I caught sight of the seated figure illuminated by the dim light.
I was unable to tell if he was miles away in my world or inches away
in a distant world.

I approached the dark figure, knowing that his eyes had felt my
presence but were occupied and could wait to meet my nearing figure
with a familiar face. Then, he raised his head slowly from the drawing
in his lap, his soft dark eyes focusing on mine as he gave a slight nod
and a gentle smile, acknowledging me with a few muffled words in
Spanish. I studied the face and noticed the subtle details. He was
barely thirty, but his face was creased with lines of struggle, pressed
into a clay mask by many hard years. His dark countenance transported
me through time to a place where I stood in front of a noble Aztec
leader.

I had come to this land to experience a different culture, to learn a
foreign language, and to encounter new people. I had arrived in his
studio like a blank canvas: he had found it, stretched it, and prepared
it for the transformation that would soon take place. With a gentle hand
he had lifted his paintbrush from his palette, and passionately sweeping his brush across the canvas, he had created a new composition in
me. He then carefully handed me the new painting, and with it, his
palette and paintbrush, still holding the paint he had used. I left con-

taining the shades of his world and holding the tools needed to face my world.

His eyes shaded by memory, he had told me with humble pride the stories of his people. He had recounted his struggles, his fighting in the revolution, and his combat in the countryside of Chiapas. He had described the oppression he and his family had suffered from the government, all with the gentle breeze of hope blowing through his words.

He had looked at me one day as we both sat hunched over our sketchbooks, and whispered in his lingering Spanish a single thought: even if things did not change, even if his hope was not fulfilled, he still had something that no government could take away, something that was his own and would wither away only after he had breathed his last breath. His soul was his, and he wanted to share it through his artwork.

My mind floated back into the cave, where it blinked, rubbed its eyes, and soared above the scene. The scene had two figures facing each other, inches away in place and time, but years away in experience, slowly connected inwardly as they proceeded in being amidst each other, joined by a connecting truth and by the soft light which threw its buoyant flicker over the two masses, distorting and twisting them into infinite and amorphous shapes wavering on the muted wall.

ANALYSIS

This is an example of how an essay doesn't necessarily have to tell something about the author forthright. Although he succumbs occasionally to the use of clichés, Tessler is talented at writing, and he exhibits this talent unrestrained in a piece at once mysterious and engaging. It doesn't try to be an ordinary essay, nor does it try to sneak in a list of achievements. Tessler constructs the essay as though it were a painting, filling it with detailed color and showing—not telling—everything he observes and imagines, unafraid to delve into the abstract.

Subtle aspects of Tessler's writing style produce a sense of enigmatic fantasy which emphasizes his ability to write and yet may confuse the reader. The first paragraph sets the stage for the essay by casting a "clouded dream" of confusion even on the part of the author, unsure of who is in what world, vacillating between the conscious and subconscious. And in the last paragraph, he separates his mind from himself and refers to this mind in the third person. Through such techniques, he envelops the reader in his imagination. The story is likely to be different from most college essays and would help instill a lasting impression on his critical readership.

Unfortunately, some might find this mystery to be too extreme. Certain fundamental ideas, such as where Tessler is and with whom he is interacting, are unclear. And the point of the essay seems lost if one does not consider the exhibition of writing style and imagination to be a major aspect of the piece. This may be to Tessler's disadvantage if the admissions staff reading this essay is left more in a state of bewilderment at what the essay was about than of admiration at Tessler's writing aptitude.

For the most part, however, the reader is likely to be left with a sense of satisfaction after reading this work, particularly due to its unusual nature. Taking the risk of slightly confusing the reader, in this case, is not inadvisable. If the reader is confused, the writing style will certainly make up for this. And if the reader is not confused, the essay succeeds in strengthening Tessler's application.

—Ronald Y. Koo

MOLDING IDENTITY

"A Formation of Self"

By Ariel Y. Perloff, who attended a small private school in
Oakland, California.

Before even touching the camera, I made a list of some of the
photographs I would take: web covered with water, grimace reflected in the calculator screen, hand holding a tiny round mirror where
just my eye is visible, cat's striped underbelly as he jumps toward the
lens, manhole covers, hand holding a translucent section of orange,
pinkies partaking of a pinkie swear, midsection with jeans, hair held
out sideways at arm's length, bottom of foot, soap on face. This, I think
is akin to a formation of self. Perhaps I have had the revelations even
if the photos are never taken.

I already know the dual strains the biographers will talk about,
strains twisting through a life. The combination is embodied here: I
write joyfully, in the margin of my lab book, beside a diagram of a
beaker, "Isolated it today. Beautiful wispy strands, spider webs suspended below the surface, delicate tendrils, cloudy white, lyrical, elegant DNA! This is DNA! So beautiful!"

I should have been a Renaissance man. It kills me to choose a field
(to choose between the sciences and the humanities!). My mind roams,
I wide-eyed, into infinite caverns and loops. I should fly! Let me devour
the air, dissolve everything into my bloodstream, learn!

The elements are boundless, but, if asked to isolate them, I can see
tangles around medicine and writing. The trick will be to integrate
them into a whole, and then maybe I can take the photograph. Aahh,
is it already there, no? Can't you see it? I invoke the Dedalus in me,
everything that has gone into making me, hoping it will be my liber-
ation.

Music is one such element. The experience of playing in an orchestra from the inside is an investigation into subjectivity. It is rem-

iniscent of Heisenberg's uncertainty principle: the more one knows the speed of a particle, the less one knows its position. Namely the position of the observer matters and affects the substance of the observation; even science is embracing embodiment. I see splashes of bright rain in violin arpeggios fading away in singed circles, a clarinet solo fades blue to black, and a flute harmony leaves us moving sideways, a pregnant silence, the trumpets interrupt with the smell of lightning. Perhaps in the audience you would sense something else.

I think of rowing as meditation. Pshoow, huh, aaah; Pshoow, huh, aaah. I can close my eyes and still hear it. We glide over reflected sky . . . and lean. And defy the request for "leadership positions," laugh at it, because it misses the entire point, that we are integral, one organism. I hear the oars cut the water, shunk shunk; there are no leaders.

Once I heard an echo from all quarters. "Do not rush," said the conductor, "follow the baton." "Do not rush," said the coach, "watch the body in front of you." Do not rush.

I write about characters' words: how they use words, how they manipulate them, how they create their own realities; words used dangerously, flippantly, talking at cross purposes, deliberately being vague; the nature of talking, of words and realities. Perhaps mine has been a flight of fancy too. But, come on, it's in the words, a person, a locus, somewhere in the words. It's all words. I love the words.

I should be a writer, but I will be a doctor, and out of the philosophical tension I will create a self.

ANALYSIS

This essay is a good example of an essay that shows rather than tells the reader who the author is. Through excited language and illustrative anecdotes, she offers a complex picture of her multifaceted nature.

The writing is as fluid as its subject matter. One paragraph runs into the next with little break for transition or explicit connection. It has the feel of an ecstatic stream-of-consciousness, moving rapidly toward a climactic end.

The author is as immediate as she is mysterious. She creates an intimate relationship with her reader, while continuously keeping him/her "in the dark" as she jumps from one mental twist to another.

She openly exposes her charged thoughts, yet leaves the ties between them uncemented. This creates an unpredictability that is risky but effective.

Still, one ought to be wary in presenting as essay of this sort. The potential for obliqueness is high, and, even here, the reader is at times left in confusion regarding the coherence of the whole. Granted the essay is about confluence of seeming opposites, but poetic license should not obscure important content. This particular essay could have been made stronger with a more explicit recurring theme to help keep the reader focused.

In general, though, this essay stands out as a bold, impassioned presentation of self. It lingers in the memory as an entangled web of an intricate mind.

—Erin D. Leib

"An Incomplete Story"

By Hilary Levey, who attended a small parochial all-girls high school in Bloomfield, Missouri.

During the Middle Ages, a ritual existed which dictated how an individual introduced himself or herself. This introductory process was threefold: first, it demanded that the individual's religion be named; next, the individual's town or community was stated; and finally, the family name was said. Even today, this method of introduction can be effective in conveying the character or identity of an individual. If I were to introduce myself, I would simply state that I am a scholar (learning is my religion); I am a contributor to the greater well-being of my community; and my family will be determined by my future plans and goals (since family includes, but is not limited, to blood relations).

While my gender is extremely important to me, I first identify myself as a scholar because intellect does not have a sex. Knowledge transcends gender. Therefore, I am a thinker, a learner, and a scholar. To me, the process of learning is religious. Words are my "bible," teachers are my "priests." I respect and revere words like others respect, revere, and fear the idea of God. I understand that words are alive and I must wrestle them down and tame them in order for them to become my own. Hence, I make it a habit to collect words. Then, like bangles and crystals that possess psychedelic and prismatic qualities, I hang the words in my mind for illumination. The meaning of my precious words are revealed to me by teachers—not just those who have a "teaching certificate," but those who awaken my mind, who ignite my senses, who alter my perception of the world; together, as Walt Whitman says, we "roam in thought over the universe," seeking to enlighten ourselves and one another.

The college experience, as I perceive it, in addition to it being the next stop on my journey for self-enlightenment, is to be the crescendo of my intellectual revolution catalyzed by professors who can awaken my mind, ignite my senses, and alter my perception of the world. I hope that my perception of the world will be slightly turned on its head and that I will be made to defend my beliefs and experience the true meaning of intellectual discovery. Thus, my only real expectation for college is to be challenged. I look upon the next four years of my life as an opportunity; I can either seize the chance and significantly better myself through the accumulation of new knowledge or I can merely go through the paces, achieve good grades, but never really feel the excitement of the words themselves. Obviously, I am looking for the former scenario—a place where mental gymnastics are applauded.

But mental contortions should not be done just for the sake of doing them; rather, they should be understood and applied to everyday life. For this reason, my quest for self-enlightenment is not limited to the sphere of academics because the college experience itself is not limited to classes—it is the formation of the complete individual, which means developing both social and academic personalities. I have confidence that the people I will meet in college will show me and share with me their enormous zest for life. This extended family will help me to forge my identity as a scholar, as a contributor to my community, and as a member of a family.

But neither my family nor my extended family nor my teachers could comprise my entire identity. Rather, I will remain like the first page of a book with the first line incomplete—a story waiting to be told.

ANALYSIS

Levey's essay is very much a self-exploration of being an intellect. Her idea of emphasizing her love of learning is solid and she clearly has a sophisticated grasp of prose, but the overall package might have done better with a little more understated elegance. The introduction is intriguing with the use of an unobvious historical fact about customs in the Middle Ages. Hilary successfully introduces herself and her perception of her role in the world. The first two paragraphs are an easy read, except that the use of too many polysyllabic adjectives can become a little bit distracting. Personal essays that are "show me rather than tell me" tend to be more convincing. What mental gymastics has she experienced before? Where has she really pushed for self-growth? The section which describes college as "the next stop on my journey for self-enlightenment" and "the crescendo of my intellectual revolution catalyzed by professors who can awaken my mind, ignite my senses, and alter my perception of the world" is a little bit over the top. You don't have to tell the reader that college is the next step in intellectual growth, the reader should be able to sense it from the essay itself.

—Jennifer 8. Lee

"Growing Up"

By Chris Shim, who attended a public high school in
Mercer Island, Washington.

I'm short. I'm five foot five—well, five foot *six* if I want to impress
someone. If the average height of American men is five foot ten, that
means I'm nearly half a foot shorter than the average Joe out there.
And then there are the basketball players.

My height has always been something that's set me apart; it's helped
define me. It's just that as long as I can remember, I haven't liked the
definition very much. Every Sunday in grade school my dad and I
would watch ESPN Primetime Football. Playing with friends at home,
I always imagined the booming ESPN voice of Chris Berman giving
the play-by-play of our street football games. But no matter how well
I performed at home with friends, during school recess the stigma of
"short kid" stuck with me while choosing teams.

Still concerned as senior year rolled along, I visited a growth spe-
cialist. Pacing the exam room in a shaky, elliptical orbit I worried,
"What if I've stopped growing? Will my social status forever be marked
by my shortness?" In a grade school dream, I imagined Chris "ESPN"
Berman's voice as he analyzed the fantastic catch I had made for a
touchdown when—with a start—the doctor strode in. Damp with nervous sweat, I sat quietly with my mom as he showed us the X-ray taken
of my hand. The bones in my seventeen-year-old body had matured. I
would not grow any more.

Whoa. I clenched the steering wheel in frustration as I drove home.
What good were my grades and "college transcript" achievements
when even my friends poked fun of the short kid? What good was it to
pray, or to genuinely live a life of love? No matter how many Taekwondo medals I had won, could I ever be considered truly athletic in
a wiry, five foot five frame? I could be dark and handsome, but could

I ever be the "tall" in "tall, dark and handsome"? All I wanted was someone special to look *up* into my eyes; all I wanted was someone to ask, "Could you reach that for me?"

It's been hard to deal with. I haven't answered all those questions, but I *have* learned that height isn't all it's made out to be. I'd rather be a shorter, compassionate person than a tall tyrant. I can be a *giant* in so many other ways: intellectually, spiritually and emotionally.

I've ironically grown taller from being short. It's enriched my life. Being short has certainly had its advantages. During elementary school in earthquake-prone California for example, my teachers constantly praised my "duck and cover" skills. The school budget was tight and the desks were so small an occasional limb could always be seen sticking out. Yet Chris Shim, "blessed" in height, always managed to squeeze himself into a compact and *safe* fetal position. The same quality has paid off in hide-and-go-seek. (I'm the unofficial champion on my block.)

Lincoln once debated with Senator Stephen A. Douglas—a magnificent orator, nationally recognized as the leader of the Democratic Party of 1858 . . . and barely five feet four inches tall. It seems silly, but standing on the floor of the Senate last year I remembered Senator Douglas and imagined that I would one day debate with a future president. (It helped to have a tall, lanky, bearded man with a stove-top hat talk with me that afternoon.) But I could just as easily become an astronaut, if not for my childlike, gaping-mouth-eyes-straining wonderment of the stars, then maybe in the hope of growing a few inches (the spine spontaneously expands in the absence of gravity).

Even at five feet, six inches, the actor Dustin Hoffman held his own against Tom Cruise in the movie *Rainman* and went on to win his second Academy Award for Best Actor. Michael J. Fox (5'5") constantly uses taller actors to his comedic advantage. Height has enhanced the athleticism of "Muggsy" Bogues, the shortest player in the history of the NBA at five foot three. He's used that edge to lead his basketball team in steals (they don't call him "Muggsy" for nothing).

Their height has put no limits to their work in the arts or athletics. Neither will mine.

I'm five foot five. I've struggled with it at times, but I've realized that being five-five can't stop me from joining the Senate. It won't stem my dream of becoming an astronaut (I even have the application from NASA). My height can't prevent me from directing a movie and excelling in Taekwondo (or even basketball). At five foot five I can laugh, jump, run, dance, write, paint, help, volunteer, pray, love and cry. I can break 100 in bowling. I can sing along to Nat King Cole. I can recite Audrey Hepburn's lines from *Breakfast at Tiffany's*. I can run the mile in under six minutes, dance like a wild monkey and be hopelessly wrapped up in a good book (though I have yet to master the ability to do it all at once). I've learned that my height, even as a defining characteristic, is only a part of the whole. It won't limit me. Besides, this way I'll never outgrow my favorite sweater.

ANALYSIS

"Growing Up" follows the form of discussing a physical or character trait, and exploring its impact on one's life. Shim's strategy is for the reader to understand his frustrations with his height, a physical characteristic that has played a great role in the way he sees himself among his family, friends, and peers.

This piece works because it is to the point, honest, and straightforward. The opening, "I'm short," delivers a clear message to the reader of the essay's main idea. As the essay progresses, Shim reveals his personal feelings and aspirations. He gives us a window into the very moment of discovery that he would no longer be able to grow. We are taken on a tour of what makes Shim tick. Being short has shaped and influenced his outlook on the world, yet it has not diminished his goals. It is personal, yet remains positive. He recognizes both the benefits and negatives of his short stature and is able to convey them in a thoughtful manner. Furthermore, the essay not only lets us into Shim's thoughts on being small but tells us his varied interests in politics, space exploration, sports, and the arts. Shim hasn't just told us how his height "doesn't limit him." He has shown us why.

—Daniel A. Shapiro

"Myung!"

By Myung! H. Joh, who attended a large public school in
Marietta, Georgia.

The hot-blooded Spaniard seems to be revealed in the passion and
urgency of his doubled exclamation points . . .
—Pico Iyer, *"In Praise of the Humble Comma"*

A re you a member of the Kung! tribe?" is a commonly asked question when people see my signature, which has an exclamation
point at the end of it. No, I am not a member of any tribe, nor am I
putting the mark at the end of my name to be "cute." In is not simply
a hiccup in my handwriting; it is there for a specific reason. But before
I elaborate on why I believe the exclamation point is such an appropriate punctuation mark for me, let us explore the other marks I might
have used:

Myung?

Although the question mark bears a certain swan-like elegance in
its uncertain curves, it simply does not do the job. While it is true that
I am constantly discovering new things about myself and changing all
the time, I know what I stand for, what my weaknesses and strengths
are, and what I would like to get out of life. I know that I want to major
in English, attend graduate school, learn as much as possible from
those who are wiser than I, and eventually teach at a university. I am
headed for a career in English; there is no question about it.

Myung,

I admit that I do pause and contemplate decisions before leaping
in and rushing ahead of myself—spontaneity is perhaps not my strong
point. But the comma, with its dragging, drooping tail, does not ade-

quately describe who I am, because I know that life will not pause for me; nor do I want it to. Amid the chaos of a hectic schedule that balances clubs, activities, and AP courses, I always feel the rush of life, and I love it. I do not linger over failures; due to my passionate nature, I am crushed by disappointments, but I move on. No prolonged hesitations or pauses.

Myung:

I constantly look forward to the surprises that college and my future life promise me; graduation seems like the beginning of a whole new chapter. But the colon, though I will not deny its two neat specks a certain professional air, does not do me justice. I know how to live for today, have fun, and enjoy life instead of just waiting for what the next chapter may bring. The future is unpredictable. My present life is not simply the precursor to what may follow.

Myung.

Perhaps this is the most inaccurate punctuation mark to describe who I am. The drab, single eye of the period looks upon an end, a full stop—but with the greater aspects of my education still ahead of me, me life is far from any kind of termination.

Myung!

However, the exclamation point, with its jaunty vertical slash underscored by a perky little dot, is a happy sort of mark, cheerful, full of spice. Its passions match mine: whether it be the passion that keeps me furiously attacking my keyboard at 4:50 in the morning so that I might perfectly capture a fantastic idea for a story, or the passion that lends itself to a nearly crazed state of mind in which I tackle pet projects of mine, such as clubs or activities I am especially devoted to.

One of my greatest passions, my passion for learning, engenders in me a passion for teaching that I plan to satisfy fully as a professor. I want my students to feel the aching beauty of John Keats's words, his drawn-out good-bye to life. I want them to feel the world of difference in Robert Frost's hushed "the woods are lovely, dark and deep," as opposed to his editor's irreverent "the woods are lovely, dark, and deep." I want them to feel the juiciness of Pablo Neruda's sensually ripe poetry when he describes the "wide fruit mouth" of his lover. With the help of my exclamation point, I want to teach people how to rip the poetry off the page and take it out of the classroom as well. I want them to feel poetry when they see the way the sharp, clean edges of a white house look against a black and rolling sky; I want them to feel it on the roller coaster as it surges forward, up, as the sky becomes the earth and the ground rushes up, trembling to meet them; I want them to feel it in the neon puddles that melt in the streets in front of smoky night clubs at midnight. I want them to know how to taste life!

My exclamation point symbolizes a general zeal for life that I want to share with others. And I know that it has become as much a part of me as it has my signature.

ANALYSIS

This essay uses a small punctuation mark to make a big point, loudly and forcefully. It answers the question "Who are you?" in a notably creative, exciting, and elucidating manner. Through an unconventional presentation, the author manages to captivate the reader's attention, while informing him/her of substantially revealing personal qualities. The strong, energized voice that is used delivers both a general, palpable sense of enthusiasm and a glimpse into specific ways that it manifests in the author's life.

The technical writing in this essay demonstrates skill. Each paragraph expresses one idea with cogency and brevity. A personified punctuation mark is presented through an interesting image and is then related to in light of the author's character. The final lines of each paragraph then cleverly bring a close to the ideas presented therein.

Though the addition of an exclamation mark could be seen as gimmicky, the author demonstrates that she has the energy and thoughtfulness needed to back up her unusual choice, in real life and on the page. It is obviously not a decision she has made lightly, nor just to make her application stand out, although one gets the impression that Myung! would stand out in any crowd, regardless of her name. It's a risky move, but for her, it works.

—Erin D. Leib

"Pieces of Me"

By Sandra E. Pullman, who attended a public high school in
Rye, New York.

The black and white composition book is faded, and the corners
are bent. It doesn't lie flat as many paper clips mark favorite
places. Almost every sheet is covered with writing—some in bold
handwriting hardly revised, others uncertainly jotted down completely
marked up and rewritten. Flipping through the thin pages, I smile,
remembering. From careless thoughts to passionate prose to precisely
worded poems, this journal marks a year of my life as a writer.

In junior year, my English teacher asked us to keep a journal for
creative writing, as a release from otherwise stressful days. We were
free to write on any topic we chose. From then on as often as I could,
I would steal away to the old wooden rocking chair in the corner of my
room and take time off to write.

As I now try to answer the question of who am I for this essay, I
immediately think of my journal.

I am a writer.

My writing is the most intensely personal part of me. I pour my heart
out into my journal and am incredibly protective of it. It's difficult for
me to handle criticism or change rejection:

i can tell he wouldn't read it right wouldn't let the meaning sink into
him slow and delicious it would sound awful through his careless
eyes i want him to open himself up to it and let in a piece of me i
want him to know this side of me no one ever has i want him to be
the one to understand let me see he prods once more i tell myself
this time i'll do it i let myself go but as it passes into his rough
hands i see it for the first time it's awkward and wrong just like me

i snatch it back from him and crumble it it falls with hardly a noise
into the trash

I am a child.

Growing up, I would always ride my bike over to the elementary
school across the street and into the woods behind it. Crab apple trees
scented the fall air and the winding dirt paths went on forever. I'd drop
my bike at the base of a tree and climb as high as I could. All afternoon
I would sit in these trees whose branches curved out a seat seemingly
made just for me.

One day I biked across the street to come face to face with construction trucks. Those woods are now a parking lot. I cry every time
I see cars parked where my crab apple trees once stood:

He allowed the sweet sadness to linger
as he contemplated a world
that he knew too much about.

I am a daughter, a cousin, a great-niece.

My family is very important to me. My mother has a huge extended
family and we all get together once a year for a reunion. I play with
my little cousins and toss them in the air to their squealing delight.
Many of my relatives are elderly, however, and I find it hard to deal
with serious illness in these people I love. I am also deathly afraid of
growing old and losing all sense of myself. When visiting relatives, I
have to come to terms with these feelings:

With the toe of my sneaker, I push at the ancient pale yellow carpet.
Like all the items in the apartment, it is way past its prime. It is
matted down in most places, pressed into the floor from years of
people's shoes traversing back and forth. It will never be as nice as
it once was, that much is certain. At home it would be pulled up,
thrown out, not tolerated in an ever-moving young family, not fitting
in with all the useful, modern surroundings. But here, in this foreign,

musty apartment where my great-aunt and uncle have lived so long
that they seem to blend right into the faded wallpaper, the carpet is
a part of the scenery. It could not be removed any more than the
floor itself.

I am a friend.

I will always treasure memories of sleep-away camp and the friends
I fell in love with there. Many of these people I have managed to keep
in touch with, but I regret that some I have lost:

But now . . . the weather is changing. A cold front has moved in.
The picture is barely noticed. Perhaps other pictures of other memories brighter and newer hide it from view. A cool breeze steals in
through the open window, and the careless wind knocks down an
old picture from the bulletin board. The picture falls in slow motion,
taking with it a far-off memory. It comes to rest behind the desk,
lying on the floor, never to be seen again. Its absence is not even
noticed.

I am an incurable romantic.

Leaving a party one night, I forgot to return the sweatshirt I had
borrowed:

touching the small hole
in the bottom corner
and the stray thread
unraveling the sleeve
I lift it up
and breathe in its smell
I smile quietly
it smells like him

I am a dreamer.

I often sit in class and let my imagination take me wherever I want to go. I love to read stories of mythic Camelot or the legendary Old South, losing myself in my favorite books:

the three dimensional
kaleidoscope fantasy
of far-off lands
and courtly kingdoms
of passion and romance
and high seas adventure
is shining with vivid colors
and singing with non-stop noise

My journal from eleventh grade not only chronicles a year of my life, but it tells the story of who I am. It is the closest I can get to even beginning to answer that difficult question:

tell them she says just tell them who you are let them know what makes you tick tick tick the clock is counting down I can't wait to get out of here just a few more minutes smile and pretend you care tell them who I am in 358 words double-spaced 12 point font as if I even know as if I could even if I did on a single sheet of paper why I cry why I laugh why I want so badly to go to their lovely school

I guess I do know one thing about who I am.

I am a writer.

ANALYSIS

"Pieces of Me" is an admissions essay with attitude—a personal statement that takes a risk.

Like many college applicants, Pullman is interested in writing. Her essay stands apart from the pack because she doesn't simply tell the admissions officer she likes to write. Instead, she used excerpts from her journal to *show* the admissions officer how much she loves to write, how much she depends on her writing to help her explain and understand life.

But Pullman's decision to include creative writing—e.e. cummings style—in her personal statement is not a decision for the meek of heart or the semi-talented. Every high school senior has heard stories of college applicants who, in the quest to stand out among the hundreds of other essays an admissions officer must sort through, submitted an original screenplay, musical composition, or videotape of an interpretive dance as their personal statement. In cases like Pullman's where real talent shows through, those risks may pay off. For others, a more conventional piece with a strong, clear thesis and well-written supporting arguments may be the better road to take.

Of course, no piece is perfect, including Pullman's. As original as many of her journal excerpts may be, Pullman prefaces many of them with somewhat cliché transitions which weaken the underlying premise of the piece—that Pullman's unique writing help articulate her unique personality. Her creative writing is exciting and interesting; her more academic writing is less so.

Still, "Pieces of Me" is a risky endeavor that works. Pullman succeeds, without the use of a 3-D visual aid or live performance, in making her application stand out.

—Georgia N. Alexakis

"Mosaic"

By Laure E. De Vulpillières of France, who attended a large public high school in suburban Paris that also had a private American section.

I **see my life as a mosaic.** There are many glistening, colored pieces shaping themselves into what will become the big picture of my future life. Parts of that picture are already in place. My favorite subjects have to do with language and culture, with history, politics and international relations, with writing and public speaking, with environment and human rights.

I love class discussions in English. It is such fun to ponder every word and debate its meaning. I love the sense of "oh, wow!" after finding a link, a theme or a symbol in a passage. My eyes get a little wider. When I excitedly tell the class of my discovery, we all enthusiastically scribble my idea into the margin of our texts. Their input excites me, too. One girl will share her insight; the boy next to me will give another dimension to that thought and then the intellectual, quiet girl in the back row will reluctantly suggest her idea, which breaks the complex phrase right open . . . and then we all think, "oh wow!"

Our French class last year was just as interesting. Our teacher had us read over thirty literary texts of about 20 lines each. Her perceptiveness was amazing! For each text, she would identify three to five themes which she discussed up to four hours. At first, I was overwhelmed by the richness and variety of her insights and had trouble keeping up. Later, though, I was able to recognize those themes even before we started the discussions, analyzing the intricacies and appreciating the care that the authors put into crafting phrases.

I've had five years of Spanish, but I really fell in love with the language and culture during my four trips to Spain. Like Americans, the Spanish are open and welcoming to visitors. Like the French, the Spanish have an incredible ancient culture of which they are not only proud, but extremely knowledgeable. On a visit to Spain with my parents, a priest overheard us speaking French and came over to welcome us. Then he spent an entire day sharing the history and treasures of his village with us. His progressive religious beliefs, his warm sense of humor, his encyclopedic knowledge and his patient concern about our understanding his country presented Spain to us in ways that could never be learned in a classroom.

I have always been fascinated by history. I remember the disbelief that I first felt at the realization that so much had happened before I was even born. The Egyptians had built the pyramids, Tito had resisted the Soviets, Algeria had declared independence from France and it had all been done without my help. My childlike ego took a hard blow. However, I remain captivated by this past this is imposed upon us at birth. With a wealth of intricate detail, my history teachers have outlined significant events from all angles to help us understand each nation's strategies and hopes. They have taught me how our past shapes our minds, lifestyles, loyalties . . . and our future.

I enjoy math, I really do . . . once I understand it. I had some problems last year because my teacher was impatient when I asked questions. However, my teacher this year is encouraging. She says my level is good and she thinks I will get an A on the math section of the Baccalaureate. I am thrilled (and relieved)!

One day I read a scientific news article about gene technology and found I understood it, thanks to my class in biology. Until then, I had never realized how relevant my biology class is to me. Now I am fascinated and pleased that I can read a wide variety of scientific articles, especially when they have to do with my interest in the environment.

Physics is not interesting to me. As terrible as that sounds, I am not at all interested in calculating the speed of a ball that falls 3 meters to the ground or in estimating how many times it will bounce. Physics is too dry, too meticulous, and has nothing to do with people.

Sit in any classroom almost any day of the year and you will hear the sound of nose blowing, coughing and sneezing. The students at any school are not a healthy bunch. There is a good reason for that. Most focus only on academia, disdain their bodies, smoke regularly and hate to exercise. I have stopped telling people at school that I jog before school to keep in shape. They just don't understand why I think it's such a *great* way to start the day.

For three years, I took judo and Chinese boxing. I learned to focus my inner energy, to connect with my opponents' energy and to use this energy against them (for example, in upsetting their balance). Now, I often use this focusing technique when I want to convince someone of my ideas.

During the entire week, I look forward to our two hours of Model UN debates after school each Wednesday. I relish my transition from mere student to important world leader. It is all a simulation of course, but we Model UN-ers enjoy the seriousness of the debates, following protocol to the letter. On subjects of great importance to the future of international relations, we become true delegates, fighting for acceptance of our country's point of view.

Five years ago, my older brother started me thinking about environmental protection when he quoted scary examples of environmental destruction. Eager to spread my new knowledge, I was happy to see a sign announcing a new Ecology Club. However, at the first meeting, I found that the organizing teacher and I were the only ones there. We were both disappointed no one else had come, but we talked about recruiting other people and organizing activities. One week later, my efforts had brought in twelve participants. Since then, countless volunteers have helped organize events, raise money and spread the word about how each of us can protect the environment.

Last summer, at the National Young Leaders Conference in Washington, D.C., I and 350 other enthusiastic students spent two weeks listening to famous speakers, participating in simulations of Congress and the Supreme Court and learning about the U.S. government. On Capitol Hill, I met a government teacher from California who was interning for his congressman. Learning I was from France, he offered to show me around. For three hours, he plunged into a fascinating explanation of the human side of Congress. For example, after emphasizing how the animosity between political parties slows the democratic process, he expressed excitement because, for the first time in a long time, Republicans and Democrats had worked together on a bill to balance the budget. I felt right at home because the politics reminded me of Model UN.

I often feel compelled to write about horrendous events that are not well-covered in the media. It really bothers me that unsuspecting readers might believe that the subjects in the news are the only important ones. For example, I am shocked that, until recently, the horrifying famine in North Korea had received so little attention or that few know about the oppression of women in Afghanistan who are not even allowed to see a doctor when they are ill. In *Crosscurrents,* we cover issues such as these in the hope that a well-informed student body will eventually spread the news to larger groups, if not to the entire world.

In theater, I love acting like someone I'm not. Paradoxically, it helps me learn more about myself. I believe that each character in a play represents a different side of us: the romantic, the heroic, the tragic, the haughty, the jester, the innocent. We may have repressed these traits in ourselves, but acting demands that we express them freely—no matter how stereotypical, complex, sad or ecstatic the character is. We must first identify these same emotions within ourselves and then express them convincingly so that the audience can empathize with our character. When I act, I have the impression that my character's emotions have been thrust into my body, allowing me to experience feelings that I've never known in real life.

As a volunteer at our local animal shelter, I look forward to sharing my time with lonely dogs. I choose four or five dogs to take on a long walk through the forest. I teach them to recognize their names, come, sit, and lie down. If I have time, I brush their coats: I really want them to look their best so that they will get adopted. I hope they are a little happier because of my small contribution.

ANALYSIS

De Vulpillières's technique in "Mosaic" is to break her life down into its many pieces and to show the different facets of her personality, her myriad interests, and what is important and even not so important to her. "Mosaic" does an excellent job of painting a detailed picture of De Vulpillières and examining all her different sides. As this is an additional essay, the extended-list format works quite well, even though it is an unconventional and possibly risky approach. Because of De Vulpillières's exceptional writing ability and her fascinating life, this essay is very unique and truly excellent. However, a list format for a main essay might be precarious, and should most likely be reserved for supplementary essays. De Vulpillières's primary essay was about her experience at The Hague International Model United Nations.

The main strength of "Mosaic" lies in the fact that it is so eloquently written, particularly considering that De Vulpillières is an international student from France. She also lets her sense of humor peek through in several occasions, such as in her paragraph entitled "I enjoy math, I really do . . ." One of the most striking aspects of De Vulpillières's essay is her intellectual curiosity and ability. Her paragraphs about her fondness for history, class discussions held in English, and her trips to Spain reflect her love of learning and of constantly challenging herself. De Vulpillières is also courageous enough to comment on many things that she does not like, such as physics, and what she is determined to change, such as the media's lack of coverage of many "horrendous" world events. One particularly outstanding paragraph is the one in which she explains her reasons for loving acting in theater productions. Her life, from this essay, is truly fascinating and lively, showing to the reader her many passions—for the environment, stray animals, Model United Nations and politics, exercise and good health, acting, etc. "Mosaic" shows us who De Vulpillières is, and that she deeply cares about many important issues.

The only true weakness in this essay is that it occasionally becomes self-righteous. The paragraph about exercising seems slightly judgmental of her fellow students: "I have stopped telling people at school that I jog before school to keep in shape. They just don't understand why I think it's such a *great* way to get in shape." Despite that one minor shortcoming, "Mosaic" is a superbly well-written essay, extremely interesting, and, un-like most college essays, gives the reader a deep insight into who De Vulpillières truly is, what she cares about, and impresses us with her world-liness, enthusiasm, and intelligence.

—Marcelline Block

"Myself"

By Jamie Smith, who attended a small private high school in
Houston, Texas.

*A teenage girl, JAMIE, walks out on stage alone from stage left. She
has brown hair that falls to her shoulders and deep blue eyes. She
is wearing a white blouse and blue jeans and in her right hand is a pair
of binoculars. The stage is dark except for a single spotlight following
JAMIE across the stage. When she reaches the center, she sits down on
the edge of the stage, her feet dangling over, and raises the binoculars
to her eyes. She proceeds to stare at the audience through them for a
few seconds, then slowly moves them away from her face.*

JAMIE: With these binoculars I can see each one of you on an
extremely personal level. *(She brings the binoculars to her eyes then
down again.)* Do any of you audience members by any chance have
your own pair handy? *(scanning the audience)* I was afraid of this. Well,
here, why don't you take mine for a while? *(She jumps off the front of
the stage, hands a front row audience member her pair of binoculars,
then resumes her previous position.)* Now look through those and tell
me what you see. Be honest now, I could use a good session of constructive criticism. Wait, maybe if I stand up you could get a better
look at my true self. *(She stands and gracefully turns around.)* Make
sure you get every angle now. Okay, now tell me everything you know
about me . . . not much to tell, is there. I mean, you really don't know
what kind of person is standing up on this stage in front of you blab-
bering on about binoculars and constructive criticism. Well, I guess I
have my work cut out for me today; I must describe who I am. Fortunately, I did come prepared. I have provided myself with a prop—and
the influence of a very special person—to assist me throughout one of
the most difficult performances of my life, an interpretation of a piece
I call "Myself." *(She steps off the stage and returns to the audience*

member in the front row.) Do you mind if I take these back now? *(She returns to the stage.)* The one prop is, you guessed it, a pair of binoculars. Not just any binoculars, they are one of the few reminders I have of my great-grandmother, Gran. No, she wasn't an infamous spy at large during World War II nor was she an avid birdwatcher. In 1986, when I was six and she was ninety-four we both watched Halley's Comet make its celestial appearance through these binoculars. I remember she said that she and I were truly blessed because we both were able to see Halley's Comet twice in our lives. She told me about seeing it out in her backyard in 1909, when she was the same age I am now. There we were together, seventy-seven years later, watching the same comet shoot across the same sky. I think of all the things that have happened during those seventy-seven years, the triumphs and setbacks Gran achieved and endured, and it has given me strength to deal with the challenges in my own life. I imagine how much life had changed since 1909 and wonder how my life will change by the time I see Halley's Comet again. What will I become? I will not, like Gran, be a part of the Oklahoma land run or witness the birth of the automobile. I will probably not be quarantined for tuberculosis or listen to the progression of two world wars over the radio. But I know I will do and be something. And the determination and success of my great-grandmother will help me reach this something. She is more than a memory or a story, she has become a part of me: my family, my history, my source of knowledge and my source of pride. Her struggles and achievements are reflected in mine. She is with me when I rise and fall and always there to make sure my feet are still on the ground. She is with me backstage and with me in the spotlight. She is a woman. She is my great-grandmother. And that's truly what she is—great, grand, everything. Gran. It's amazing how a simple name can inspire so much.

She sits down, returning to her initial position with her feet dangling over the edge. She brings the binoculars to her eyes and looks through them. But instead of looking at the audience, she is attempting to look beyond them, almost as if there is some invisible sky behind the rows of seats. She slowly moves the binoculars away from her face, but her eyes are still fixed on some object off in the distance.

JAMIE: Only sixty-six years to go. I've got to make them count.

ANALYSIS

Written in the format of a play script monologue, both in style and overall structure, this essay addresses the concept that it is difficult to evaluate a person from strictly superficial appearances. In order to truly know someone, no matter how closely you study their outer appearance, it is what's inside that counts. Emotions, thoughts, dreams, and personal goals are the most important and telling aspects of one's identity. The writer does not just theorize about such ideas, but makes a logical progression by giving a concrete, vivid example to back up her thesis. Without having to explicitly list interests or personality traits, the style of the essay reveals a good deal about the applicant: she probably enjoys acting or playwriting and is highly creative and optimistic about life.

One of the strongest aspects of the essay is the fact that it is written as a monologue. The creative format is going to stand out from the thousands of other application essays that admissions officers must read. The use of binoculars as a linking device between the present and the past is highly effective—it produces an overall coherence within the essay. The applicant's use of a very specific moment to frame her love for "Gran" increases the naturalness of the passage. In many cases, essays written about family member can sound contrived. The use of a specific event adds to the realism of the applicant's emotion. The creative use of stage directions addresses the adage "show—not tell" head-on. It is an effective way of creating a mental picture of the applicant in a reader's mind. The essay also ends strongly as the last line clearly identifies that the applicant is ambitious, hard-working, and eager to make something out of her life.

The monologue of the essay is effective, but it is important to point out that such attempts to be overly creative can backfire. This applicant's familiarity with this style of writing is apparent. If you attempt to write your essay in a nonstandard manner, make sure you have a similar comfort level with the techniques you are using.

—Joshua H. Simon

"Who Am I?"

By Michael Cho, who attended a small, all-male, suburban high school outside of Cleveland, Ohio.

I wish I could write about the Michael Cho who stars in my Walter Mitty-like fantasies. If only my personal statement could consist of my name followed by such terms as Olympic athlete, master chef, boy genius, universal best friend, and Prince Charming to every hopeful woman. These claims would be, at worst, outright lies, or at best, gross hyperbole. My dreams, however, take their place alongside my memories, experiences, and genes in the palette that constitutes who I am.

Who am I? I am a product of my reality and my imagination. I am innately depraved, yet I am made perfect. I plan my day with the knowledge that "Everything is meaningless" (Ecclesiastes 1:2), but I must "make the most of every opportunity" (Colossians 4:5). I search for simple answers, but find only complex questions.

Once, on my way to a wrestling tournament, I was so engulfed in thought over whether living in an abode which rotated near the speed of light would result in my being younger (utilizing the Theory of Relativity) and stronger (utilizing the properties of adaptation along with the definition of centripetal and gravitational force) that I failed to realize that I had left my wrestling shoes in my locker. My mother says that my decision to wrestle is indicative of the fact that I don't think.

Through working in a nursing home, the most important lesson I've learned is that I have many lessons yet to learn. Thus the most valuable knowledge I possess reminds me how little knowledge I have.

Oftentimes people make the mistake of assuming that mutually exclusive qualities bear no relationship to one another. Not so! These dichotomies continuously redefine each other. In some cases one is totally dependent on the other's existence. What is faith without doubt? Without one, the other does not exist. When juxtaposed, opposites create a dialectic utterly more profound and beautiful than its parts. Walt Whitman embraces this syncretism by stating, "Do I contradict myself? Very well then I contradict myself, (I am large, I contain multitudes)." My qualities, though contradictory, define who I am.

Although I can't make fantastic claims about myself, I must still acknowledge and cherish the dreams that I have. Admittedly, it is tragic when one is so absorbed in fantasy that he loses touch with reality. But it is equally tragic when one is so absorbed in reality that he loses the ability to dream. When a healthy amount of reality and fantasy are synthesized, the synergy is such that something beautiful will undoubtedly result.

ANALYSIS

This applicant addresses the proverbial question of "Who Am I?" In doing so, he expresses, both implicitly and explicitly, his hobbies, extracurricular activities, and outlook on life. The writer not only reveals his participation in wrestling, work at a nursing home, and knowledge of Quantum Mechanics, but he also exposes the reader to many aspects of his personality and inner thoughts on life. His questioning of the meaning of life and evaluation of his own identity reveal an inquisitive side to his personality.

Overall, this essay is well written and easy to read. The introduction is strong in that the applicant levels with admission officer by admitting he does not consider himself to be a spectacular individual, giving the impression that what follows is written honestly. Another strong point of the essay is that it reveals many of the activities in which the writer is involved. This serves to give the admissions officer a more personalized picture of the applicant. The biblical and Walt Whitman quotations are very well used and demonstrate the strong intellect of the writer.

While the essay does provide some insight into the philosophical thoughts of the applicant, in many ways it is too theoretical. The writer could improve the essay by specifically listing the dreams or goals he cherishes or perhaps by writing in more detail about one of the many experiences he mentions in the statement. The flow of the essay is also hindered in a number of ways. First, the word choice seems slightly unnatural—almost as if the applicant relied on a thesaurus when writing the essay; as a result, the tone seems to be a bit contrived. Second, while the overall theme of self-identification is maintained throughout the essay, the individual paragraphs jump from one topic to the next in a disjointed fashion. For example, it is interesting to know that the applicant worked at a nursing home, but mentioning such does not seem to fit with the overall progression of the essay. It is important that the personal statement convey to the admissions officer a sense of who you are and what you are like in person, but it is not necessary to cram every extracurricular activity or accomplishment into the essay; there are other sections of the application for listing such things.

—Joshua H. Simon

"My Name"

By Uyen-Khanh Quang-Dang, who attended a public high school in Santa Clara, California.

W endy!"
          I was walking down the hallway, my shoulders sagging from the weight of my backpack nearly bursting with books on the way to a student council meeting, from the worries of the canned food drive, from all the thoughts which cluttered my brain just moments before. I sank into a deep thought about the two names, Wendy and Uyen-Khanh.

My parents, my grandmother, and all my peers at the Sunday Vietnamese Language School knew me as Uyen-Khanh, my name as written on my birth certificate. Yet I was a wholly different person to my "American" friends and teachers—I had always been Wendy. Even some of the award certificates I received read: "Wendy Quang-Dang."

Wendy is an invented name bestowed upon me by my kindergarten teacher who decided that Uyen-Khanh was too difficult to pronounce. In fact, it became so convenient that I began to introduce myself as Wendy to avoid the hassle of having to slowly enunciate each syllable of "Uyen-Khanh" and hear it transformed into "won-ton" or "ooh-yen kong." It was especially hard on substitute teachers, who would look up from the roll book, flustered and perplexed as they tried their best not to completely destroy my name. Wendy also greatly decreased the looks of terror and embarrassment as people would struggle to remember how to say "Uyen-Khanh" two minutes after we had been introduced.

But at that moment standing alone in the hallway, I decided that I wanted to be known to all as one person: Uyen-Khanh. Wendy had served me well for the past eight years since kindergarten, but it was time I let go of a nickname and recognized the name written on my birth certificate.

It took me over three months of consistent persistence and patience to erase the name so many had known me by. Letting up on my determination to brand Uyen-Khanh into everyone's memory for even just a second was not a possibility if I wanted my mission to be successful. This meant pretending not to hear someone calling me unless it was some form of Uyen-Khanh. I would interrupt people mid-greeting and stand my ground when my friends would glare angrily at me and whine, "But I've always known you as Wendy!" My philosophy was that people must respect my wishes to say Uyen-Khanh. By the end of those three long months my resoluteness had paid off and I was richly rewarded by the sound of Uyen-Khanh pronounced smoothly and effortlessly by my closest friends.

I was thirteen years old born and raised in San Jose, the second largest Vietnamese populated city in the United States. A first-generation Vietnamese citizen of this country, English was as native to me as the language of my ancestors, Vietnamese. I grew up a "true American," as my grandmother would call it, for I did not just adapt to the all-American lifestyle, I lived it. When I decided to shed the name casually given to me in kindergarten, it seemed to some that I was "going back" to my true heritage, believing that being called Uyen-Khanh would somehow make me more Vietnamese. The truth was I was more "American" then ever when Uyen-Khanh replaced Wendy. Being born and raised in San Jose as a first-generation Vietnamese citizen made me who I am, a Vietnamese-American. Uyen-Khanh was just the name I was given at birth, and it was simply time to acknowledge it.

ANALYSIS

Uyen-Khanh's essay falls squarely into the "identity" category, as the writer tells the story of defining her American identity by deciding to force her friends to call her by her given name, Uyen-Khanh, rather than a long-held American nickname, Wendy.

The writer expresses the difficulties she experiences and the persistence necessary to change the way she is viewed by her peers and teachers while stealthily squeezing in several allusions to her life as a busy student ("student council meetings," "Vietnamese Language School," and "canned food drives"). These allusions are so well integrated that her essay doesn't lose its flow or sense of direction, in fact, they show that she is very much the "true American" she says she is in the text.

This essay's greatest strength is in its style. Neither flowery nor over-written, the essay is simple and straightforward without being formulaic or trite. Uyen-Khanh efficiently tells the story of her name and links that to her identity as a Vietnamese American person at once deeply appreciative of her Vietnamese heritage, but every bit an American. She does a good job of moderating her stance so that what could have been an angry treatise shows her to be firm and compassionate. It shows her to patiently refuse to yield when friends try to revert to her nickname, but at the same time allowing them time to get used to pronouncing her given name. All together this is a solid essay with good tone, pacing and language.

There are few weaknesses to speak of in Uyen-Khanh's essay; if any-thing she may have missed some opportunities to further expand on her description of herself as a Vietnamese American. Every college essay is a compromise of thoughts and space as one tries to strike a comfortable balance between self-promotion and reflection. Ultimately, this essay re-flects numerous good choices and results in a success.

—Jason M. Goins

"Modern-Day Hobo"

By Chad Callaghan, who attended a small private school in
Gates Mills, Ohio.

With the gift of a wooden pull-train on my first Christmas, trains
and model railroading entered my life, full steam ahead. What
were wooden and plastic toys are now sophisticated metal engines and
detailed cars. "O," "G," "HO," and "N" gauges, LGB, Atlas, Athearn,
Mantua, Rivarossi, Spectrum, Pola, 2-8-8-2, shay engine, turnout,
spur—are now a familiar vocabulary. Track sprawls across the train
room floor, requiring an awkward dance of tip-toeing and side-stepping
to get from one side to the other. This is a world unlimited by the
room's four walls and track geometry.

The trains allow me to deal with ideas and problems that are not
academic or theoretical. Is this coupling better than another? Is that
an authentic paint scheme? Are those wheel flanges in gauge? Is this
the right ballast for the track bed? What's the history of this engine?
Did it pull freight or passenger cars? Would this train fit into my
modeling scheme of railroads east of the Mississippi River before
1950?

My hobby has also taken me out of the train room, to the real thing.
For me, travelling by train is fun because it is s-l-o-w. I like to meet
other people with the same interest in trains—people who agree that
enjoying the trip is often more important than getting to the destination.
Whether it was riding the "611" (one of the most streamlined steam
locomotives ever built) from Cleveland to Columbus and the Ohio State
Fair, trying to find a non-smoking car on a Canadian train from Toronto
to Montreal, riding the "Chunnel" train under the English Channel
(the train broke down for six hours in a small tunnel in the English
countryside—we really got to know our fellow passengers!), or taking
the rapid transit downtown to an Indians baseball game, I remember
the people and the good-time feeling of going somewhere together.

Model railroading is a great diversion. The attention required to assemble the small parts of a model, or the repetition of cleaning the cars, removes me from the events of the day. As the trains speed around the loops of track, they wear away the day's deposits of cynicism, exhilaration, disappointment, and pride. Solving a wiring problem or assembling a new station building gives me a great deal of satisfaction. Tomorrow's discussion in English class, the math test scheduled for the day after vacation, the piano piece to memorize, the yearbook deadline, my grandfather's ill health—all melt away for a few hours.

My model railroad is constantly beginning. There is always a hill to redesign, a station to move, a section of track to rework. Perhaps it is the lack of boundaries, the freedom from facts and analysis, the opportunity to use my imagination in ways not possible during day-to-day activities that make me return to my model trains.

For hobos of yesteryear, railroads provided a means for escape and change. Hopping on a train opened the door to opportunity and possibility. With this in mind, I suppose I am a modern-day hobo of sorts. Instead of riding the rails to find a fresh start, I journey along with my imagination through the world of model trains, and I am ready to begin again.

ANALYSIS

Writing about a hobby is a risky business. Success means sharing one's enthusiasm without seeming overbearing or tedious. Callaghan succeeds because of his great gift for description. He does not insult the reader's intelligence as he presents his material, nor does he compromise the readability of his essay with cumbersome and esoteric details. Callaghan makes it easy to imagine enjoying what he enjoys, with a winning blend of fact and anecdote. He skillfully alludes to other interests (piano, yearbook) without spreading himself too thin.

—Matthew A. Carter